Denys Parsons

KU-485-452

FUNNY AMUSING AND
FUNNY AMAZING

Pan Original
Pan Books London and Sydney

First published 1969 by Pan Books Ltd,
Cavaye Place, London SW10 9PG
6th printing 1983
© Denys Parsons 1969
ISBN 0 330 02338 1
Printed and bound in Great Britain by
Cox & Wyman Ltd, Reading

INTRODUCTION

The success of *Funny Ha Ha* and *Funny Ho Ho* has encouraged me to compile yet another volume of the exploits of Gobfrey Shrdlu. Still nobody has disputed my claim that Shrdlu is the evil genius who inspires all the misprints and howlers which plague authors, printers, and sub-editors. He also has a hand in bringing about certain strange happenings, oddities, freak accidents, and absurdities which are reported in the Press.

As usual I have arranged, for your enjoyment, howlers and misprints (Funny Amusing) on the left-hand pages, oddities and absurdities (Funny Amazing) on the right-hand pages.

My thanks are due to the editor of *Weekend* for permission to include material, and to many others who have waived copyright. Particular thanks to Mr Edward North of Sidcup who has again contributed many items.

Readers of my *It Must Be True* series of six Shrdlu books will perhaps forgive me for including a number of the best items from those books which were published by Macdonald & Co. in the 1950s.

Funny Amusing

Funny Amazing

Can you provide hospitality when a mixed party visits Newbury for Festival Week? Offers with preference for sex, will be gladly received by Mr L. Jackson.

Newbury Weekly News

And sometimes, bodice backs need to be of average size while the fronts must be made for outside bosoms.

Sheffield Star

But the Yorkshire men stuck to their gins with great determination and kept themselves well in the game.

Huddersfield Weekly Examiner

Repairs to the Town Clerk are completed and the Borough Surveyor reported that the fitters would be assembling the parts this week.

Cambrian News

A stolen cello worth £3,000 was last night returned to its owner, Mr Anthony Pini, principal cellist of the Coventry Garden Orchestra.

Daily Mail

Graham Stilwell, one of this year's Wimbledon heroes, was involved in another match on Saturday – his wedding. Graham, with his partner, Whipps Cross Hospital, met his lovely bride while on tour in North America three years ago.

Stratford Express

If you are absent from work owing to illness or injury on the date on which you join the Plan (or, if this is a non-working day, then on the next preceding working day) you will not be entitled to the death benefit until you return to work.

from a firm's Retirement Benefit Plan

Laboratory tests have shown that a curry meal had caused a shorthand-typist to give out a form of dye which made everything she touched turn pink.

Dr Valentine Crowley, medical officer at the Chrysler Cummins factory, Darlington, said yesterday: 'This was a phenomenon I had never come across before. Something in her system reacted against turmeric in the curry and sent something like pink dye through her pores.'

The Guardian

His Lordship said that the consumption by fire of the mortal remains of homo sapiens was not the subjection of goods and materials to a process within section 271 (1) (c) of the Income Tax Act, 1952.

The Times

PADDED BRAS, wigs, and false eyelashes are to be included under a Florida law as goods that 'alter the appearance of any package to deceive one as to the actual contents.'

The People

DRIVE TO BAN HORSE WHIPPING MUSHROOMS
Headline in *Dominion*, Wellington, NZ

(Here Gobfrey Shrdlu has put us in a tantalizing flutter of speculation. Was it this crazy horse who started whipping the mushrooms? Or was it a sinister cluster of horse-whipping fungoids that had aroused the wrath of the New Zealanders? We shall never know. – D.P.)

Completing an impressive ceremony, the Admiral's lovely daughter smashed a bottle of champagne over her stern as she slid gracefully down the slipways.

Provincial Magazine

Batteries, no deposit; tyres, small deposit, six months to repent.

Evening News (Bolton)

The Judge will have the power to order off any dog that commits a fragrant error.

Gowerton & District Annual Show Schedule

All this is being investigated today by the Scottish Society for the Prevention of Cruelty to Animals and Glasgow police.

Glasgow Evening Times

Young lady required to work in accounts office, previous experience not essential bust must be able to type.

Provincial Paper

In an Everton attack, Royle was injured and lay writing in the centre of the field.

Middlesex Paper

The World's Seven Great Crises. Saturday, 13th May to Thursday, 25th May. God willing (Friday excepted).

Cwmbran New Town Advertiser

Can one eat curtains?

No, in general one cannot; but it may be as well to say what happened to an experienced housewife. She wanted to wash her curtains. They were delicate, so she went about it with care, but there was no indication as to how they ought to be washed.

Was it the way she set about it, or the washing compound she used whose composition she did not know? Anyhow her curtains turned into a kind of soft paste, something like cream cheese, which she put in a bowl to show to her husband. Then she went out to do her shopping.

As luck would have it, her husband returned before her, looked for her in the kitchen, and getting hungry while waiting, he cut a slice of bread to eat with this sort of cream cheese on the table.

'Even with plenty of salt and pepper, your cheese is quite insipid,' he said to his wife on her return. . . He retired to a night of anguish, and without even getting indigestion.

If textiles do not carry a label specifying precisely how they should be washed, should they not be marked 'eatable' or 'uneatable'?

> translated from *J'achète mieux*,
> the Swiss equivalent of *Which?*

Monsieur Nardin, a wealthy Frenchman of Lyons, was ordered to pay an excess charge he had disputed with the French Post Office. He retaliated by buying a plot of land high up in the Alps and building a chalet on it. He then installed a tenant and subscribed to a Paris daily paper.

The nearest post office was twenty-five miles away, but each day the paper had to be delivered. The postal authorities tried to cancel the arrangement but failed. In the end Nardin won. The Post Office refunded the excess charge in return for the cancellation of the newspaper subscription.

> *News agency story*

'Some mental associations were almost instantaneous,' she said. 'Henry the Eighth and Hampton Court were always linked together in one's mind, just as were Louis Fourteenth and Vera Sailles.'

> Surrey Women's Institute bulletin
> quoted in *Evening Standard*

The marriage suffered a setback in 1965 when the husband was killed by the wife.

> *The New Law Journal*

A warning should be given about Cat-Scratch Disease. The disease spreads involving swelling and puss formation.

> *Sarawak Tribune*

Although there are estimated to be 50,000 different kinds of living insects, only 60 species are definitely known to be disease carriers. Enormous quantities of these are exported by New Zealand, during one season she sent to Britain 85,000 tons.

> Malay paper

If you asked six friends to name the commonest bird in Britain, the odds are that nine out of ten would say the sparrow.

> *Weekend*

Seventy guests attended the honeymoon in the Rampsbeck Hotel.

> *Penrith Observer*

For the artist, the problem of commission is that the man who commissions it may not like the finished job. This need not always be quite such a ludicrous state of affairs as that so wonderfully described by Barnett Freedman when he told of an artist friend of his who had just completed a portrait for an old lady. She said that she did not really know whether she wanted to have it until she had seen whether her cat liked it and could she bring her cat to see it. The artist said of course she could; he would like to make a few finishing touches before the artistic cat had a chance of seeing it. As soon as the old lady had gone he smeared the portrait over with kippers and the cat was, of course, extremely pleased. The old lady took the portrait.

from *Paying the Piper* by Trevor Russell-Cobb

A man who uses pebbles for grinding stones into cosmetics powder has been told he can remove 350 tons of pebbles a year from Chesil Bank, on the Dorset coast, only if he replaces them with an equal tonnage of 'approved pebbles'. The removal of too many pebbles has led to severe winter flooding.

Daily Telegraph

IRRESISTIBLE. That is what a 63-year-old man thought when a mini-skirted girl sat next to him on a bus. He bit her thigh. And was jailed for three days at Belo Horizonte, Brazil. His comment: 'The Pope was right. Mini-skirts are dangerous.'

Weekly paper

Police in Corpus Christi, Texas, answered an emergency call from an angry housewife and found they were expected to arrest her husband, who was indoors, drunk.

When they pointed out that he had a perfect right to be drunk in his own home, the wife dragged her husband into the street. The police then arrested him.

Reveille

Her soft, lilting Irish voice conjured up the misty mountains of Mourne and the tumbling waters of the Liffey. Unmarried mother, 90, with an 8-year-old daughter . . .

London Weekly Advertiser

Fifteen-foot travel trailer. Boat rack built on top and wench for loading.

Kern Valley Sun

Mr George Dobbs, of Chertsey, is very proud of the fact that he walked 50 miles on a sausage sandwich at the weekend.

Staines and Egham News

Hammers: Bulk purchase. Suit home handymen with claw heads.

Advert in *Lancashire Evening Post*

BRITISH FLY
TO DISCUSS
PROBLEM PIPELINE

Headline in *The Sun*

Believing that good pictures are both lovely in themselves and a necessary complement to good furniture, she has a wide range of oil pumps to suit all tastes and pockets.

Advert in *Reading Evening Post*

THE GREAT MOUSE MYSTERY

Sir, – From time to time, magazine writers review the celebrated mystery of the sealed Vault of Barbados, where heavy lead-lined coffins were found to have been disturbed on several occasions between 1807 and 1819, the cause never having been elucidated. Perhaps you could help to elucidate a new mystery – the Barbados mice.

Our first mice were all caught, conventionally and easily, in cheese-baited traps. But then our mice began pushing the trap-trigger up instead of down, and so ceased to get caught.

Well, my wife got so mad that one day she asked our handyman what to do. Normally she asks only the expert, and asks warily, but she accepted his advice quite eagerly.

'Cheese isn't no use. You should bait with ham.'

We don't usually eat ham, but my wife bought some and we had the inevitable sandwiches, and the mice were offered the leavings. They pushed them up and ate them. Just as they had done the cheese. My wife told the handyman, who insisted that ham *was* the right bait. So we ate more sandwiches . . . and the mice pushed up more ham and consumed every scrap, in total safety.

I suppose that might have been the end of the matter, if a mouse had not got shut one night in a new cupboard and gnawed his way out, ruining the door. When my wife really makes up her mind her expression does not change, rather does her whole body warn all concerned. The mice did not heed!

She baited the trap with *beef*. I was sitting typing, as I am now, with the trap behind me in the kitchen, when SNAP. I called out: 'By golly we've caught one! It must have tripped over the trap.' 'Nonsense,' my wife said. 'It's the beef.'

I disposed of the carcase and she re-set the trap with the same sliver of beef, and I went on typing. SNAP. She seemed to be right. Next evening she seemed even more certainly right, for the same morsel of beef caught another mouse.

Two questions arise: what causes mice to push cheese and

ham, but pull beef? Will our next mice pull beef? Or pull cheese? Or pull ham? Or push all three?

One doesn't expect consistency in humans, but I had in the past found animals pretty reliable. Perhaps I just haven't had enough experience with them.

Anyway, here we are near town and near the sea, with our apartments all new and clean and ready for letting, and we're determined to keep the mice out, even if we have to bait with steak. Brian Smith, Waterford House Apartments, Christchurch, Barbados.

Letter in *New Scientist*

Returning to his parked car, Mr D. A. Stoddard, of Atlanta, Georgia, discovered the battery had been stolen and the petrol tank drained. He went to the garage to buy another battery and more petrol, and returned to find the front two wheels missing. He went away to buy two spare wheels and returned to discover that the whole car had vanished. Reporting his loss to the police, he learned that a policeman, seeing the partly stripped car, had assumed it had been abandoned and made arrangements for hauling it away. *News agency story*

Presumably any person on a bicycle who charges into an old lady is neither passing nor overtaking her but merely striking her and would not be guilty of an offence.

Mr Robin Turton on the Countryside Bill

The £ was looking lovely yesterday – £17 2s worth of it written all over the bare midriff of Margaret Hall. Housewife Margaret, 24, wearing a bikini, became a real live cheque and was paid into the National Provincial Bank at Sutton, Surrey. The money, collected by a motoring club, will help handicapped children through International Voluntary Service.

At the bank, assistant manager Arthur Hannah put the official stamp on Margaret. Then the details of cheque No 02127024 were fed into a computer – and Margaret went home.

Daily Mirror

Sir, The first time I heard the cuckoo was on April 12th. Flying overhead from the garden, my husband heard it before that date.

Western Gazette

'We're not back-pedalling, quite. It was apparent to us that unmarried mothers were in a rather special category. It was felt we would rather deal with them individually than under an umbrella. This rule was brought in to possibly save the council from a possible embarrassing situation.'

Slough Observer

You could have a portrait of yourself or your child taken at the convenience of your own home.

Advert in *The Times*

Six girls struggled from sickbeds on Tuesday and downed their swimsuits for a last-minute rehearsal for the final ceremony.

Straits Times (Singapore)

It is with regret we learn of the sudden death of Donald Everett, of Durris, and wish him an early and complete return to full health.

Aberdeen Evening Express

The Ministry of Agriculture is easing restrictions imposed after foot-and-mouth outbreaks in Hampshire. The infected area around Arthur Jones, solicitor, was reduced at midnight.

Portsmouth Evening News

WEST BERLIN: Horst Beck, 36, an hotel porter who searched wastepaper baskets for East German security agents, was jailed for 18 months by a West Berlin court.

Daily Mail

A seventeen-year-old Copnor youth was remanded in custody to Portsmouth Quarter Sessions by Portsmouth Magistrates yesterday after he had admitted stealing three bicycles, a record player, thirty-one records, a National Insurance Card, and two cases of false pretences.

Portsmouth Evening News

Wanted:
EDIBLE OIL
TECHNOLOGIST

Advert in *The Observer*

Going overseas? Emigration, Business, or lust pleasure. Immediate passages available.

Advert in *Liverpool Echo*

1928 ROLLS-ROYCE HEARSE, original body, 43.3 hp. Excellent condition. Box No 68 c/o P - - - & Co, Norwich.

Advert in *The Times*

Wanted. As a result of a recent Rural Dean's Visitation, the Parish of Westwell urgently needs a safe measuring approximately 30 in by 24 in. Offers please to the Vicar, Westwell Vicarage, Ashford, Kent.

Canterbury Diocesan Notes

Strangest blaze in a Dorset fire brigade report: A man stubbed his cigarette out on his plastic false teeth – and started a blaze in his bedroom.

The People

Two fish tanks for sale, one fish tank with stand, complete with fish, one box of fish knives and forks.

Leicester Mercury

The judge rejected a petition by 50-year-old Mrs Roberts alleging cruelty.

Among her allegations was that, 20 years ago, her husband, a shipwright, slapped her round the face with a wet fish.

The judge said: 'If one slap with a wet fish in 40 years of marriage is cruel – and I don't consider that it is – then that cruelty has, in any case, been forgiven.'

Daily Sketch

While trying to become a stockbroker he developed the unfortunate tendency of wanting to dress as a woman.

News of the World quoted in *New Statesman*

A member of the African Family Planning Association said: 'We are having a lot of trouble with pregnancy in secondary school girls, and this represents a lot of man-hours wasted.'

Medical News

WILSON – Treasured memories of a dear mother and grandma, who passed away August 3rd, 1967. In God's garden of heavenly rest, Lies one of the dearest, And one of the best. – Jack and Emma and all at Asplin garage. £3,100 or near offer.

Scunthorpe Star

Amid the cheers of their many friends in the farming community the bride and groom cut the wedding cake made by Mrs Luston (shaped like a haystack on stilts).

Dayton, Ohio, paper quoted in *Evening Standard*

Up to 13 lbs dry weight for only 2/9 including soap

Blankets 1/9 each including soap

Old Age Pensioners 2/- including soap (special days).

Leaflet from Laundry and Dry Clean Centre

The possibility that the gang would try to smuggle the gold to India or Pakistan – where gold is worth three times its value in Britain – led to a special watch at Heathrow Airport and a special check being ordered on any ship sailing there.

Birmingham paper

The tangled romance of 'D' and 'B' is an affair fraught with suspense. It unfolds slowly in the small ads column of a Lancashire evening newspaper. It is a story which rarely looks like having a happy ending.

It began on January 2, innocently enough, with the message 'Dear D, greetings. All my love, B.' Love's first storm clouds arrived on January 17 with: 'Dear D, do I deserve this? Feelings are unchanged, B.' On January 19, the tiff seemed about to be solved when 'D' replied: 'Dear B, please ring. Miss you, D.'

On February 7 the ad read: 'Dear D, how nice seeing you. One still hopes, even if hopeless, B.' Two days later the following appeared: 'Dear B, nice seeing you too. Not hopeless, D.' Then there was the advert on March 1, 2 and 4, in which 'D' repeatedly declared: 'Dear B, I think of you day and night. Love, D.' It was followed puzzlingly on March 6 by: 'My love D. If messages are yours why so unfriendly? Need you always, B.' To which 'D' replied on March 9: 'Sorry B. Did not mean to be unfriendly. Afraid to show my real feelings. D.'

A dramatic note entered the correspondence on April 2 with: 'My lovely D. Went to avoid chief. Hope to talk it over soon. Love, B.' Which brought the reply of April 5: 'Dear B, glad you explained. Thought I was mistaken. Shall we have a talk? D.'

The suspense was finally too much. The following heartcry appeared in the column last night: 'Dear D and B. Suspense is killing us. Please get on with it. Two fans.'

The Sun

Contusions of the larynx may be caused by blows or kicks, by garotting, or by a cart-wheel having passed across the neck. The affected parts are sometimes painful and there may be alteration or loss of voice.

from a Manual of Surgery

Who shall say what hereditary destiny may have in store for this small boy, whose mama is deep red, and conspicuously labelled in big letters: 'Peculiar People's Chapel.'

North country paper

In a bitterly cold wind, the Queen, wearing a warm sage-green tweed coat with a beaver lamb collar and a green mitre-installation of turbo-alternators and boilers.

Essex paper

The committee expressed the view that the school-crossing patrolman could best assist the children if he were dead outside the school entrance.

Public Service

Unaccompanied ladies
not admitted unless
with husband or similar.

Notice in Cairo bar

The raiders took about £600 in cash. 'They left nothing untouched, the whole place was a shabgm', selM'bolaletaoin in a shambles,' Mr Higgins said.

North Berks Herald

NO WATER –
SO FIREMEN
IMPROVISED

Liverpool Daily Post

Due to a misunderstanding over the telephone we stated that the couple would live at the home of the bridegroom's father. We have been asked to point out that they will in fact live at the Old Manse.

Local paper quoted in 'The Black on White Misprint Show' by Fritz Spiegl

Sixty per cent of patients in a Massachusetts hospital who conversed with the DOCTOR machine, despite being warned that they were talking to a computer, insisted that they must have been consulting a real human being. 'No machine could understand me that well.'

The Observer

It is unlikely that the defendant in a damages case brought by George Albrecht will ever appear in court. Barring a miracle that is. For the party 35-year-old Mr Albrecht is suing is ... GOD.

Mr Albrecht has filed a suit charging that God was responsible for an accident in 1964 in which he injured his back. In the suit, filed at West Palm Beach, Florida, yesterday, Mr Albrecht also named all the churches in Palm Beach county – about thirty altogether – as co-defendants. He did this because he claims the churches are 'the agents of God'.

Mr Albrecht, an electrician, injured his back during a rainstorm when a construction site sidewalk suddenly collapsed. He sued the city council and the construction company. But a jury ruled that the mishap was 'an Act of God'. Now a judge has been assigned to hear his new claim.

The Rev E. W. Zilch, of Bethel Pentecostal Temple, one of the cited churches, said: 'I would be extremely happy to testify for the defendant if Mr Albrecht brings him into court.'

Daily Mirror

Dear Sirs,
In buying your biscuits I have noticed that the top biscuit in the packet is nearly always broken. I am therefore writing to suggest that in future you should leave out the top biscuit in each packet.

Yours truly, Mrs N. Jackson

Letter to biscuit manufacturer.

The Waltham Cross and district branch of the Family
Planning Association has now become part of a larger group
known as the Herts and Beds branch.

Medical News

GENT, 36, good looking, intelligent,
needs company lady, average build,
intelligent, 22–36, interests: cinema,
dancing, motoring, etc: marriage
later if necessary. – Write Box 1370.

Surrey Herald

Target of 25,000 tons of crab a week has been reached by
miners at the new colliery of Monkenhall.

Daily Record

Self-improvement course for women of all ages. The art of
make-up, deportment, hair styling, charm and personality,
etc, personal attention, fee for worm and dry rot.

Dublin Evening Press

Porter rubbed his nose, wondering what it would sound like,
and if it would appear as it had twenty years before when he's
taken part in it all.

from *Light Cavalry Action* by John Harris

The spare key to the First Aid Room is available in the
First Aid Room.

Notice in Government Department

A British tourist just back from Egypt found one morning that insects were hatching out of his shirt buttons. The shirt was bought in Cairo. The buttons, he learned later, were made from palm nut riddled with almost invisible larvae.

Daily Mirror

COUPLE BAR SON WHO STOLE PLASTIC GNOMES

The parents of a 19-year-old youth refused to have him back in their home yesterday after he admitted stealing a lavatory seat from them. His father would not stand bail for him.

The youth, their only child, had also taken a plastics rabbit, three plastics gnomes, a bird cage, three tins of baked beans, a watering can, a chip fryer and other kitchen utensils, and food from the house.

Daily Telegraph

Should nude ORs salute?

WHAT, some punctilious Germans have been asking, is the correct procedure when a naked soldier encounters a similarly unclad officer in a nudist camp? Those who thirst for guidance on this delicate point of military protocol should consult this week's edition of the illustrated magazine *Stern*.

In a solemn interview with the magazine, Herr Matthias Hoogen, the Defence Commissioner of the Bundestag, comes to the conclusion that the other rank concerned would be required, under present regulations, to come smartly to attention, 'bringing his right hand to the side of his head'. However, Herr Hoogen concedes that there might be a case for arguing that a nudist camp, like a restaurant, cinema, or museum, was an 'enclosed public space' where the military greeting was not necessary.

The Times (by permission)

Said a Farnborough shop-keeper, 'The Council is pulling the bread and butter out from under our feet.'

Hants paper

PEER'S SEAT BURNS ALL NIGHT

. . .

Ancient pile destroyed

Wilts paper

Every year during Cowes Week a lunch party is held aboard his Dutch barge. A special guest at this year's party will be 17-year-old Paris schoolgirl Marie T - - -. Mr L - - -, a member of the Stock Exchange, a lieutenant in the RNVR, and also a member of 15 yacht clubs, bought her in 1958.

Evening News

The bus came to rest with its front two feet in the air.

Sheffield Star

Hall with kitchen and toilet (can seat 100 persons), or could be converted for dwelling house.

Edinburgh Evening News and Dispatch

Whichever method is used for cleaning the dog's paws, make sure that the paw is thoroughly washed with lukewarm water and is thoroughly dried. Spread with cream cheese. Place 2 or 3 asparagus tips on each and sprinkle on a little cayenne pepper.

South Wales Gazette and Newport News

GIANT SNOWBALLS – TO MAKE THE DESERTS BLOOM

Headline in *Evening Standard*

In his 20 years as a Japanese dentist, Yoshitaka Kawahara has pulled 60,000 teeth. To commemorate his work, he has buried 54,000 of them and built a tooth-shaped memorial above them.

Tit-Bits

WORLD'S FATTEST MAN DIES AT 32 COFFIN TOO BIG FOR CHURCH

New York, July 11 (France-Soir) – The fattest man in the world, Robert Earl Hughes (age 32, 75 stone 12 lb) died yesterday of heart disease complicated by German measles. Too fat to get into a ward (his girth was 10ft 4 in) he was treated in a mobile 'Ward' on the forecourt of Bremen Hospital (Indiana).

The brother of the deceased has had a special coffin made. The funeral service will be held at Emden cemetery (Missouri), in Hughes' home town. There is no question of trying to get the coffin into a church.

quoted in *Bizarre* by Barry Humphries

KEEPING DRIER IN THE RAIN

Mathematical rules have now been devised to allow pedestrians to remain as dry as possible when caught in a shower of rain. The calculations were reported in *Nature* yesterday by Mr M. Scott, a mathematician at Durham University.

When walking into the rain one should lower the head and walk as fast as possible. When the rain is coming from behind one should either walk forward leaning backwards, or backwards leaning forwards, at a deliberate pace. These methods guarantee a moist rather than wet walk.

Sunday Telegraph

Undiminished Activity of Queen Mary
Altering the Lbw Rule

The Guardian

TO THE FAIRY GLEN

Five minutes walk

BEWARE HEAVY LORRIES

Notice in North Wales

The day was slightly marred by a hold-up caused by a serious accident and later fine rain with sausages.

Hampshire parish magazine

DIAMOND LIL DEAD

Claremont, California. Diamond Lil, once famous show-girl who had nine husbands and diamonds set in her front teeth, died here aged 89.

Daily Mail

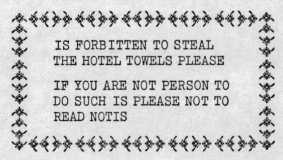

```
IS FORBITTEN TO STEAL
THE HOTEL TOWELS PLEASE

IF YOU ARE NOT PERSON TO
DO SUCH IS PLEASE NOT TO
READ NOTIS
```

Notice in Tokyo hotel

The cook at a Swiss hotel lost a finger in a meat-cutting machine and put in a claim to his insurance company. The company suspected negligence and sent a representative for an on-the-spot investigation. He asked to be allowed to work the machine – and lost a finger. The cook got his insurance money.

Weekend

Four policemen surrounded 26-year-old chef Alan Williams when he got off a train at Shoreham, Sussex, yesterday. A report telephoned down the line had said that a man carrying a gun in a shoulder-holster was on the train. 'Hand it over,' said one of the policemen, pointing to the bulge in Mr Williams' jacket.

Mr Williams fumbled inside his jacket and produced – a fish. 'I bought it for my cat,' he explained. 'I was in a hurry and stuffed it inside my jacket.'

Mr Williams of Woodview, Shoreham, said last night: 'It was a frightening experience – quite a crowd gathered. I realize the police were only doing their duty.'

The Sun

A prime cause of the poultry industry's £5 million a year loss on cracked eggs was explained yesterday by Dr T. C. Carter, director of the Poultry Research Centre in Edinburgh: Some hens stand on tiptoe to lay – and consequently their eggs drop harder to the floor.

Daily Express

'I wish he wouldn't wear his old sports jacket – it makes him look a freak,' said Mrs Omi, wife of Brighton ex-officer showman who wears a 3-inch ivory ring in his nose, 5-inch daggers in his ears, and is dyed blue all over.

Daily Express quoted in *New Statesman*

Serve with fried bananas and sweet corn fritters (in to-morrow's Daily Sketch.

Daily Sketch

Todorovic went out at an early stage, but his form in training suggests that he is a highly capable performer, following a kick from a bullock.

Irish Times

The man was wearing a mustard covered V-necked pullover or cardigan, and using a large white car.

Lancashire Evening Post

This is a particularly serious offence which we have to deal with severely, as a detergent to anyone in the same mind.

Leicester Mercury

A fixture that has brought nothing but defeat since 1949 was won at last by the shooting of two Football League forwards.

Daily Mail

The report said the drugs might cause girth defects if administered to pregnant women.

Yorkshire Post

How about this for service? I took a wrist-watch into a jeweller's here in town to be repaired. On Monday I collected it. Nothing unusual in that, you might say, until I tell you when I took it to be mended.

It was twenty-six years ago! I was not then 15 years old and I forgot to collect it. Months went by and I hadn't the nerve to go in and ask for it. I left it so long I thought they must have sold it. But on Monday I had cause to go into the shop again, so I asked, on the off-chance, whether it was still there.

Sure enough, the son of the previous owner of the shop found it for me. It still had on it the ticket in my maiden name which was put on it, by his father! The jeweller said his record for holding a watch before was eight years, so he suggested I write to you about it.

I wasn't charged a penny. I think the jeweller was so surprised that I had turned up after all those years.

Daily Mirror

Whenever journalist John Montfort rings up his office, he does so literally. He has a voice in a million, which sets bells ringing along the line as soon as he speaks. The bells make it impossible for anyone on the private line at Southern Television's Dover newsroom to understand what Montfort is saying. That's not all. Sometimes the Dover office telephone bell actually starts ringing, too.

No one knew what the trouble was – until Mr Montfort, a sub-editor, working at Southampton complained to the Post Office. They analysed his voice and discovered it set up sound waves at exactly 500 cycles a second.

Last night a Post Office spokesman said: 'The frequency set up electric relays on the line and accounts for the ringing tone in the earpiece and the bell going off again.'

The chance of anyone having a voice pitched at exactly 500 cycles a second is about one in a million, said the spokesman. He added that an electrical adjustment had been made to the telephone bell at the Dover office. Now nobody is summoned by bells whenever Mr Montfort is on the line.

The Sun

> This packet of ready-made
> pastry will make enough for
> four persons or 12 tarts.
>
> .   Instructions on package

French-speaking or Continental waitress wanted for high-class West End restaurant. No undays. Very good position.

Advert in Evening Standard

The bride made her own wedding gown – a classic style in white brocade. Her train was the 6.15 pm from Redhill.

Surrey Mirror and County Post

Mrs Whelan, who can just see the top of the new cathedral from her front doorstep, added: 'Of course it's not finished yet. My son is coming round later today to put trelliswork up around the front door.'

Liverpool Echo

Said Christine, a librarian: 'They were quite polite about it all. The leader of the gang saw that I was sacred.'

Daily Express

SIDCUP (BROOKLANDS AVE) – A most attractive sd house (re-built 1948) in excell dec condition, sit in a most sought after posn on the Sidcup/New Eltham borders. Close to local shops and schools, whilst New Eltham Stn is within easy reach providing a very good service to the City and bathrm.

Kentish Independent

A MOTORIST, THE LAW, AND AN ASS

If you have a donkey beside you is it safe to drive? Magistrates at Totnes, South Devon, had to decide this yesterday when a man appeared charged with not having proper control over his small Citroen car.

Peter Cox, principal of Dartington College of Arts, Dartington, near Totnes, pleaded not guilty to the charge.

Constable Kenneth Arthur told the Court: 'As the vehicle drew near I saw the backside and tail of a donkey through the windscreen and very close to the driver. On causing the defendant to stop, I confirmed that the animal was a donkey.' PC Arthur said the rear seat of the car had been removed and Cox's wife was sitting in the back holding the halter of the donkey, which was in a standing position. The front passenger seat had been removed. The prosecution contended that Cox did not have proper control because his visibility was restricted.

Cox said the donkey was very tame. He produced a photograph showing that the driver could see between the top of the donkey and the roof of the car and to either side of the car. While he was being cross-examined the Bench stopped the proceedings and dismissed the case.

The Guardian

A Liberal undertaker writes: 'I cannot get Tories to give me any money for the Liberal Party whilst they are alive, so I am adding £1 onto their funeral expenses.'

Liberal News

☛   Weidenfeld and Nicolson, who recently published 'The Nightclerk', by Stephen Schneck, would like to remind all booksellers that the book begins in the middle of a sentence on Page 9.

The Bookseller

Dear Madam,

I am sorry that your gas installation does not give you an adequate supply of hot water. I will go into this with you as soon as convenient.

Letter from Wilts gas company

He saw that she was a woman of over fifty, wore a blue silk blouse with a frothy fissure ornamented with much lace, and the vagueness of one constantly tripping over in the habitual race against time.

from The Shadowed Mirror by Joan Medhurst

Sexi-detached Bungalows and Houses, new, £3,500.

Dalton's Weekly

A sub-committee is to consider the question of alterations at the village hall so that the toilets can be used for Football matches.

Daily Mirror

The manufacturers of this sock MUST be washed in LUKE-WARM water, NOT HOT, and well rinsed to remove soap.

Instructions with Pearlustra socks

SERVICE HAND. Mon–Fri. 10.30–3.30. £7 to serve waitresses from the hot plate. Tel: MIN 9999.

Evening Standard

DRINK TEST BEATEN BY BIG TOE

JOHN FORSTER, 23, told a doctor that he could take a blood sample from his big toe and nowhere else, Chester-le-Street, Co Durham, magistrates were told yesterday. The doctor refused. The magistrates acquitted Mr Forster on a charge of failing to provide a sample for a laboratory test.

Mr GOMER MONTGOMERY, prosecuting, said that Mr Forster, a partner in a bakery business of Front Street, Sacriston, Co Durham, was taken to the police station after a police car had been forced into the side of the road by a car belonging to Mr Forster. Dr WALLACE BEXON said that when he asked Mr Forster where he would like the blood sample to be taken from he said: 'My big toe.' The doctor told him that this was not one of the accepted places which were: the ear, thumb, or arm.

The doctor told the court: 'He refused to allow me to take a sample from any of those places. I consider that his attitude constituted a deliberate refusal to provide a sample.' Dr Bexon said he told Mr Forster that he did not wish to take a sample from his big toe because of the danger of infection. Mr RICHARD REED, defending, said: 'There would be a risk of infection wherever a sample was taken. It is not laid down anywhere in the Act that a person must give a blood sample from any particular place on his body.'

The magistrates dismissed the charge. They also dismissed a charge of refusing to take a breath test after Mr Reed had submitted that there was no evidence that Mr Forster had been driving the car.

Daily Telegraph

Mrs Fyoedor Vassilet, wife of a Russian, never had a single child. She had four sets of quadruplets, seven of triplets, and sixteen sets of twins, making sixty-nine children in all.

Reveille

He is now being kept alive by an artificial respirator and massive doses of rugs.

Nelson Evening Mail

In the final instalment of Anton Mikulencak's article in the Granger News last week, the text as printed read: 'Nobody did not see me drink here.'
It should have read: 'Nobody did not seen me drink here.' The NEWS regrets this error and is glad to make this correction.

Granger (Texas) *News*

The perfectly formed brilliant coral-red blooms are produced in great profusion and the fragrance is something to behold.

Lowes Flower Catalogue

At a meeting held in the institute last Wednesday, Mrs Davis was won by Mrs J. Hawker.

Darlington and Stockton Times

THIS ROAD IS CLOSED TO
ALL VEHICULAR TRAFFIC EXCEPT
GOVERNMENT VEHICLES AND
THOSE BELONGING TO PERSONS
HAVING BUSINESS AT PIRBRIGHT
AND NOT EXCEEDING 126in. IN
HEIGHT WHO MAY USE IT AT
THEIR OWN RISK

Sign at entrance to Pirbright Camp

Det Con E. Holmes claimed that Else bought the knife in Chesterfield on Saturday and took it to the house. He added that when charged Else declared: I didn't really attempt to murder her, I really wanted to frighten her to death.

Derby paper

CHEST FREEZERS

The top-opening chest freezer is a good choice.

The Times

To move the cabin, push button of wishing floor. If the cabin should enter more persons, each-one should press number of wishing floor. Driving is then going alphabetically by natural order. Button retaining pressed position shows received command for visiting station.

Notice in Belgrade Hotel lift

I read with interest of the lady golfer who, when confronted by a naked man wearing only a bowler hat, asked him whether he was a member, and then hit him with a Number 8 iron.

Purists will long dispute whether it was obviously a mashie-shot, or whether the niblick should have been used. I hold no strong views myself, but I do wonder what the lady would have done had the man produced from his bowler hat a valid membership card.

Letter in *Daily Mail*

The Arboricultural Association are holding a meeting in London on February 1 on the subject of Trees in Towns. Among those attending will be the secretary of the National Dog Owners' Association.

The Sun

Alderman G. Duddridge said it was no use holding a post mortem on something that was dead.

Morpeth Herald

Members of Park 60 Club were entertained by Swindon Evergreens Choir yesterday. The pianist was Mrs Smith. The conductor Mrs A. Bates were wearing prison overalls when they escaped.

Wilts paper

K - - -'s Bridal Hire. Brides from £5, with all accessories. Also bridesmaids any style made to measure.

Leyton and Leytonstone Guardian

A basement flat comprising three rooms, kitchen, bathroom, outside WC (at present occupied by owner).

House Agents' leaflet

WANTED by a reputed electrical firm a livewire sales representative on salary-cum-commission basis in Coimbatore city. Attractive terms offered for the right person having very good contacts. Apply to Box 5231.

Indian Express

In a 25-minute speech he took apart the Government's case with the artistry of a surgeon, and at the end left it scattered about the operating theatre headless and limbless.

The Times

PROGRAMME FOR OFFICIAL OPENING OF THE ABAKRAMPA PUBLIC LATRINES

1. Public procession through the streets to the latrine led by Abakrampa Brass Band.
2. Guests to take their seats.
3. Opening prayers by Rev Abonyi (Methodist Church).
4. Introduction of Chairman and other important personalities by Mr S. G. Gyandoh, Snr.
5. Music.
6. A short history behind the project by the General Secretary.
7. Address by Administrative Office (Central Region).
8. The uses of this type of latrine, by Mr Ocloo.
9. Music.
10. The sod to be cut by a representative of the NLC and inspection of the latrine by the guests.
11. Omanhen's address.
12. Vote of thanks by Clerk of Council.
13. Music.
    Light refreshment at the Community Centre.

quoted in *World Medicine*

ROLLA, MISSOURI.

Mr and Mrs Ronald Cook were on their way back from a squirrel-hunting trip. They stopped the car to buy two baby pigs and put them in the boot, along with the .22 hunting rifle.

Suddenly a shot rang out. Twenty-year old Mrs Cook cried: 'My God, it hurts.' Then she slumped dead. One of the pigs had apparently bumped against the rifle and it went off.

Evening News

Marinade the steak in the sauce for at least two hours, then cook a hot grill, basting with the sauce at frequent intervals. Alternatively, pour off sauce after marinading, heat separately, and let your guests pour it over themselves.

Recipe in Ohio newspaper

'I have scored four goals in eight games – but the shorts are not really going all that right at the moment, some of them are just popping wide.'

Evening Standard

Enjoy our large airy rooms for small families. Home-type food, diets catered for, Scandinavian pastry, home-made muffins, country fresh eggs. Hospital is the aim here.

from a travel leaflet

Thieves described by the police as 'amateurs' broke into the Shakespeare Memorial Theatre at Stratford-on-Avon, it was discovered yesterday morning, tried to open a heavy steel safe witashea-prgtp ocmfw cmfwyp safe with a stage-proprty sword and a Shakespearean statute, smashed restaurant cupboards and disturbed bar stock.

Daily Telegraph

A thief went to work in the changing room at Burtonwood Rugby Club. Honey was taken from the pockets of five players.

Ashton and Haydock Reporter

PIGEON NESTS ON GLADYS AT HYMN TIME

Headline in *Daily Mirror*

A Greek fisherman admitted in Sutherland Court last week that he had used a line nearly three-quarters of a mile long and baited with 230 hooks. When asked why he had used more than the legal limit of six hooks on one line, the fisherman had replied that he had been fishing in the dark and couldn't count the hooks.

Local paper

The pilot of a private aircraft called the control tower at Kansas City's municipal airport and said: 'You might inform the TWA plane which is about to take off from the north end that the object near my position that looks like a rock is really a turtle on the runway.'

Boeing 707 captain to control tower: Tower, we heard that transmission. Understand. One turtle crossing runway.

Control tower: Based on available pilot's report, turtle's course is oriented South-east, heading towards Gate 5.

707 captain: Kansas City tower, can you give us info on turtle's speed and estimated time of runway clearance?

Control tower: Computer calculation indicates turtle speed around 200 feet an hour – maybe less in this quartering headwind. If threatened course and speed are maintained, runway should be clear in 8 minutes.

707 captain: Unable to wait due to fuel depletion. Will employ evasive action on takeoff roll.

Control tower: Roger, TWA. Cleared for takeoff. Be on alert for wake turbulence behind departing turtle.

The story is related in the current issue of 'Skyliner', the airline's newssheet for staff.

The Guardian

GIRLS—
they could be our
answer to the
shortage of scientists

Headline in *Daily Express*

Mr Cooper found a faded picture of old brickfield workers under cobwebs in the cellar.

Slough Observer

The Manx Government plans to relax regulations on boarding houses to make more beds available for tourist sin late August and September.

Daily Telegraph

BANANAS IN SYRUP

Heat in an enamel-lined saucepan some red-currant jelly and raspberry jam dissolved in water, making a pint in all. When all boils, drop into it a dozen peeled tomatoes.

Weekly paper

Then the whole congregation joined in singing: 'Let us with a Gladstone Mind.'

Birmingham paper

£1 REWARD. Lost, an Octagonal Lady's Gold Wristlet Watch.

Advert in Wigan paper

Nathan Boya went over Niagara Falls inside a high rubber ball in July 1961. It drifted ashore on the Canadian side, where Customs officials seized it, insisting that the ball was a foreign vessel navigating inside their territorial waters.

Reveille

UNBORN BABY SWALLOWS A BULLET

A baby girl was critically ill in New York yesterday after swallowing a bullet before she was born. The bullet was fired at her mother, 20-year-old Mrs Lucy Ortiz, as she was standing at the window of her apartment on Tuesday morning. She was eight months pregnant.

Doctors said the bullet must have lodged inside the mother and been swallowed by the baby, who was born prematurely by Caesarian operation. Now they are wondering whether to operate on the 5 lb girl, critically ill with lead poisoning, or hope that the bullet will work its way out through her intestines. The mother is in 'fair' condition. Her attacker has not been found.

The Sun

When four girls were fined on charges of 'over exposure' in a show called 'G-String Revue' at a Virginia carnival, one of them challenged a woman police officer's evidence that the girl was nude. She had, she said, a G-string round her ankle.

Reveille

WILL THE ONE WHO
REPORTS THE ONE FOR
NOT SWEEPING THE
STAIRS KINDLY SWEEP
THEM HIMSELF
THANK YOU

Chalked on blackboard at Euston station

The 'middle order batsmen' have a year of struggling and grafting to stay in the swim, as they try to climb the ladder.

Evening News

If you were one of the fortunate people to attend the dinner given in May in honour of Dr Frank C. Hibbon, Director of the Anthropology department of the University of New Mexico you were fortunate.

from an American museum bulletin

Silk? Tweed? Hopsack? Worsted? No matter what your topcoat is made of, this miracle spray will make it really repellent.

Advert in Ohio newspaper

Mr A. Woolard, at the organ, rendered suitable music both before and after the wedding ceremony. The hymns were 'O Perfect Love' and 'Thin for ever'.

Islington Gazette

```
ORDER NOW YOUR SUMMERS SUIT.
BECAUSE IS BIG RUSH WE WILL
EXECUTE ALL CUSTOMERS IN
STRICT ROTATION
```

Sign in Jordan tailor's shop

Her eyes lit up, fluttered, met his, dropped to the floor, went back to the jewels. He picked them up, held them for a moment, then handed them back to her with a tender smile.

from a short story

Farmer's wife Elsie Scott has a plum tree in her living-room. The tree has grown under Mrs Scott's home – Irving House at Appleton Wiske, Yorks – and up through the interior wall between the living-room and kitchen.

A dozen 2 ft-long branches have broken through into the living-room ... giving her quite a problem when she decided to have the room papered. Mrs Scott, 55, said yesterday: 'Eventually I found a flowered wallpaper that matches the branches so that they don't show up too badly.'

Daily Mirror

Two young men begin a search today for Britain's biggest cooking pot – to boil an elephant in. Raymond Chaplin, assistant curator at an East London museum, and John Atkinson, his technical assistant already have the elephant. It has been lying embalmed in the museum's cellars for three years. They need to boil it in water and chemicals so that they can present the skeleton to the Passmore Edwards Museum at West Ham. It will be used to assist in the identification of Ice Age elephants.

Mr Chaplin explained: 'It's a very worthwhile project. A complete elephant skeleton can cost anything over £1,000. If you order one you have to wait at least two years for delivery.' The pot they are looking for should be able to take 40 gallons of water and have some form of electrical heating. Even with that size pot, they will have to 'cook' the elephant a bit at a time. A large water tank might be the answer. Mr Chaplin and Mr Atkinson would be glad to hear from anybody who has one to spare.

The Sun

Whilst building an extension to a 7-year-old hospital in Mozambique, contractors made a hole in a wall – and found a forgotten maternity ward complete with about £50,000 worth of equipment. It is believed that someone accidentally walled up the ward instead of putting in a door. There is to be an inquiry into why, up till now, no one has missed it.

Evening Standard

'I had waited so long . . . for what? For babies. That's all I wanted – to be a monster.'

Real Story

Bolting horse
saved after
fall off pony

Headline in *Daily Telegraph*

PLEASE NOTE. YOU can order our rings by post. State size or enclose string tied round finger.

Advert in Yorks paper

Roman Catholic morality is not opposed to heart transplants as long as there is absolute 'certainty of conscience' that the doctor is dead.

The Times

'Miss Lane came round some time ago collecting names for a petition,' said Mrs Jane Earls, 30, mother of two and a news-agent.

Daily Mail

The Government were strongly urged to take steps to put a stop to the growing evil of methylated spirit drinking by the Liverpool justices at their quarterly meetings.

Liverpool paper

CHINESE PUZZLE

The American woman tourist insisted on buying the material for a coat, and brushed aside the protests of the Chinese salesman. She just loved that authentic Chinese lettering on the material.

But when the woman collected her new coat and put it on, Chinese children kept following her in the street, says Gene Gleason in his book 'Tales of Hongkong' (Robert Hale, 25s). And in a restaurant everyone stared at her in amazement. They seemed intrigued by the Chinese lettering, which was across her chest. At last, the woman's husband asked a waiter to explain the characters. The translation was 'condensed milk'.

Weekend

The driver of a sports car was giving a fat woman a lift, and she stowed her handbag behind her seat. Near the end of the journey, she knelt on the seat facing backwards to pick up her bag.

The sports car driver had to jam his brakes on in a hurry . . . and the woman reversed sharply into the windscreen. She was undamaged, but the screen was a write-off.

Weekend

In October 1950 a slow race for motorcars was organized along Rue Lepic, Paris, France. The winner, M. Durand, took ten hours, forty minutes, and fifty-one seconds to drive a total distance of only seven hundred and twenty-two yards.

Timekeepers all along the route watched, ready to disqualify any motorist who stopped. They noted that at one stage Durand's wheel took nearly three minutes to make one complete turn.

Two years later another motorist went slower still. He is reported to have taken twelve hours to travel only forty-nine and a half feet.

News agency story

FOR SALE, Wicked Bath Chair, and good mahogany Bed Table.

Kentish paper

Barrie was still in the water and swimming strongly when Annal abandoned his attempt. He had still about four miles to swim as the crow flies.

Scots paper

Garsia's Law Relating
to Carriage of Goods
by Sea in a Nutshell.

Publisher's Advert

He broke into the building with an older boy, and they then splattered the walls with floor, ransacked teachers' desks, and one beheaded the school paste, tipped treacle on the goldfish with a paper guillotine.

Slough Observer

Visiting hours in women's colleges should be made equal to those in men's colleges. There is little conceivable reason for prohibiting men visitors in women's rooms.

University paper

The visit has been planned in the atmosphere of the general economy going on in the country. The lunch has been cut to the bare bones.

Daily Express

NEVER ALONE WITH A SNAKE

People sailing on board a cruiser competing in Poole Yachting Regatta this week have been keeping a weather eye open for an unusual sailing companion – a five feet long yellow rat snake. Visitors to the yacht – Tarka, owned by Mrs Nancy Curme, of South Newton, Wiltshire – are warned by a notice in the cockpit, 'Please be careful of my pet snake which lives in the boat.'

Mrs Curme said yesterday: 'The snake isn't poisonous but I put up the notice because you could never be sure of someone's reaction if they suddenly saw it sliding about below decks.' The snake, which comes from America and is called Rita, is fed on eggs and dead mice.

The Times (by permission)

The title of the film 'PLINK PLONK PLINK' (F 52377), registered on June 7, 1967, has been corrected to read 'PLINK PLUNK PLINK'.

Board of Trade Journal

Once a year for the past 18 years Ed Clinch has regularly received a fresh coconut – and he has no idea who is sending them to him. They arrive at his home in Peoria Park, Illinois, by ambulance, helicopter, police car – even by hearse.

Clinch says: 'The people who bring them all say someone leaves the coconut on their doorstep with a note asking them to deliver it to me.'

Weekend

Mr Thomas, who was stationmaster at Coleford for 10 years, has been appointed stationmaster at Cinderford.

Gloucester paper

CARS LEFT IN FRONT OF HOTEL ARE AT OWNER'S RISK

Garage in outer space available
on request.

Notice in French hotel

Why is it that tenants of Council property are treated like so many prawns on a chess board?

Louth Standard

Fourteen-year-old Victor Harris has passed with credit two of the recent Royal Academy of Music piano examinations. For failing to stop he was fined £5.

Darlington and Stockton Times

The choreographed Mass, believed to be the first ever danced round an altar in a Catholic cathedral, was watched by an audience of 1,800, including the Archbishop of Liverpool, Most Rev, Dr. George Beck, and the Lord Mayor, Mrs Ethel hit him.

Dublin Evening Herald

In a raid on Partington Railway Station during the weekend, thieves stole four dozen pencils and three dozen ball-point pen refills.

They told the 'Guardian' that their headmaster was very pleased with their success and the honour it reflected on the school.

Sale and Stretford Guardian

They won't let Valerie Braithwaite go to work by bus. All because of her job. She is a fire-eater. The trouble is that 24-year-old Valerie takes her working gear with her. And that includes a gallon of petrol. London Transport refuse to let her take the can of petrol on a bus. 'And that makes life a bit difficult,' Valerie said yesterday at her home in Neasden. 'It means I've either got to walk to where I'm giving a show – or go by taxi, which is working out very expensive.'

Valerie, who trained as a fire-eater for three years, has been appearing at dinners, parties, and in cabaret for the past year. 'Since I've got really busy, I've got to go all over the London area,' she said. 'I've explained to dozens of bus conductors that I've got to take my petrol with me, but they just turn me off. I can't even go by Tube. They won't let me through the barrier at the station.' Valerie added: 'I just don't know what the solution is. The taxis are costing me a fortune. And I can't afford a car.'

A local police spokesman said yesterday: 'According to the Public Vehicle Equipment and Use Regulations of 1958, no highly inflammable or otherwise dangerous material may be carried.' And a London Transport spokesman said: 'It's a pity about Valerie. But this is a national ruling and one which our conductors have to carry out. Under no circumstances would we allow her to carry petrol on the bus.'

Daily Mirror

The move to sell the pier started when the Rev John Payne, a Congregational minister, went down to open the town's Refugee Year campaign in January. The target was set at £500. The Mayor, Mr Edward Walker, said that in the end, to raise the money, it became a choice between selling the pier and the new public convenience at the foot of the pier. They just could not bring themselves to sell the convenience because it got a special architectural award as the best building of its kind.

The Guardian

Like Adela, he had dark brown hair, with enormous black eyebrows, a moustache, and a short beard.

from *A marriage of inconvenience* by
Thomas Cobb

'Put soap on the runners of the bureau drawers instead of jerking them in and out until they fall apart,' advises John Litwinko.
'If that doesn't help, take the Methodist Episcopal Church.'

Philadelphia Evening Bulletin

The harbour and Long Island Sound were covered thick with ice and a large number of transatlantic steamers could not get in. Traffic was almost at a standstill. In a village near New York a woman was found in bed beside her husband.

Neue Wurzbürger Zeitung

The Nebraska legislature was asked to enact a law providing annulment of marriages of all couples who do not within three years after the wedding have one or more children by Representative Hines, Democrat of Omaha, who is a bachelor.

Omaha radio news

In the women's singles semi-finals of the Victorian lawn tennis championships, Miss Turner, playing her usual baseball game, confused Miss Casals.

Birmingham Evening Mail and Despatch

NYLON CUTS THE DIET OF WORMS

The grim struggle against gribbles continues but a new British discovery promises a victory. Nylon is gribble-proof.

The gribble, and its help-mate the teredo, are ship-worms whose boring among the timbers of wooden ships, barges, and launches causes considerable damage. Methods of destroying them include chemical spraying and the experimental use of ultrasonic vibrators, reported in The Sunday Telegraph two years ago, which shake the gribbles to death. Trying preventive measures, a Southampton firm, Leicester Lovell & Co Ltd, has devised a nylon skin to be attached to the hulls of boats. It appears impenetrable both by gribbles and teredos, whose jaws recoil helplessly. One early user has been the Nigerian police force whose anti-smuggling launches have been treated. There is as yet no evidence that de-gribblization has increased the number of Nigerian smugglers caught.

Sunday Telegraph

A plane flying from Iceland to Glasgow refuelled last night at a roadside filling station in the middle of Argyllshire.

The plane, a Cessna 150, with only the pilot aboard left Reykjavik, in the morning.

Then, said a Board of Trade official last night, this is what happened:

Air traffic control at Glasgow Airport received a message from the pilot that he was lost.

Three minutes later, Glasgow received a second message that the plane had only half-an-hour's petrol left, and was landing in a field. It came down near Loch Fyne, eight miles from Inveraray, and close to a petrol station.

The pilot promptly refuelled and took off again for Glasgow, where he was said to have landed safely an hour and a half after his first message.

Sunday Mirror

Mr and Mrs Benny Croset announce the birth of a little son which arrived on the 5-15 last Thursday.

West Union (Oregon) People's Defender

Our picture shows Field-Marshall Viscount Montgommery, at a ceremony in Durham Standard in the Coronation procession to Westminster Abbeery, who will carry the Royal ex-service men at the Drill Hall, Gilesgate, yesterday. ere the Field-Marshall is talking Croix de Guerre. Viscount Montgowho holds the DCM, MM, and Town Hall, received the freedom of Durham City.

Yorkshire Post

Bachelor (40), non-driver, would accompany same on car tour of Ireland.

Belfast News Letter

Mr Barden spoke with an eloquence which sprang from his deep-seated conviction of the grave pass which we have reached, basing his proposals upon the significant memorandum which the Almighty had prepared at his request.

Montreal Gazette

Q. In breeding rabbits, is it necessary to take the doe to the buck's cage?
A. Chances of success are far greater if the doe is taken to the buck's hutch.

Weekend

Every afternoon I take my little boy of three to the park, and I like to get talking to people. There is a nice Frenchman I often chat to, and now my son is calling him Papa. I am terrified this will happen one weekend when my husband is with us. How can I stop it?

Letter in *Evening Standard*

It was a good joke and Malcolm Moyer got a lot of laughs out of it. Yesterday, however, he decided the time had come to bring it discreetly to an end. That is why the following notice went up in the restaurant of Mr Moyer's 400-year-old pub, the Ruddy Duck.

'Owing to increased local demand, my supplies of L'eau Duponde wine have dried up and I do not anticipate any further supplies.'

He included L'eau Duponde – otherwise duck pond water – on his wine list as a trap for the wine snobs. 'I caught over 50 of them in three months,' said 43-year-old Mr Moyer yesterday: 'I made it the cheapest wine in the list and the demand has been tremendous.' The wine list at the pub near the village of Peakirk, Northants, described L'eau Duponde thus: 'Matured locally. A heady wine, varying in colour with unique bouquet. It should be drunk with a pinch of salt.'

Said Mr Moyer: 'One young chap who came here for a meal even told his girl friend that it was a wonderful vintage which he once had in London. It was difficult to keep a straight face when anyone asked for it. But I always told them it was sold out and gave them something else. Now the joke's over and I've proved my point that there are dozens of wine snobs about.'

The Sun

Hunter Robert Coury, aged 23, was in hospital in Mesa, Arizona, yesterday, after accidentally shooting himself in the leg with his pistol – and then shooting himself in the other leg when he fired the gun to summon aid.

Daily Express

HYMN 326 'Stand Up, Stand Up for Jesus!'
(Congregation seated)

Michigan church leaflet

LADIES' FANCY NYLON BRIEFS
with cotton gusset,
packed 2 dozen, assorted
colours per box, will split.

Small Trader and Wholesaler

Coo forty-five minutes and cover with a layer of sliced tomatoes. Season lightly with salt and pepper and coo until meat is very tender.

Beverly Hills Shopping News

The young of the hoatzin, a curious fowl-like bird native to South America, are remarkable in having clawed fingers on their wings by means of which they are able to climb about in trees like quadruplets.

Georgia paper

FLOODING:
SURVEYOR
STEPS IN

Headline in Bristol paper

Dog's prize for composure under unusual circumstances goes this week to John Robert-Blunn, a Manchester Evening News Staffman on 'Mr Manchester's Diary.'

He was conducting a particularly careful telephone interview with an outside contact for a Diary story when he interrupted smoothly, and said: 'Pardon me, would you repeat that? Someone has just fallen through the ceiling.'

A workman helping to install pneumatic tubes for the super tele-ad department created for the Manchester Evening News had missed his footing in the roof space overhead, come through the ceiling and cascaded the Diary office with plaster and dust.

But the show went on. Diary story successfully obtained. Work on the great new tele-ad department forging ahead fast.

UK Press Gazette

Student Marian Hannay wanted to pay a university colleague the £1 she owed him. But she hadn't a cheque handy. So she wrote the cheque on an egg, and slapped a 2d stamp on to make it legal. David Blackburn, who, like Miss Hannay is studying at Nottingham University, handed the cheque into a branch of the Westminster Bank. The cashier remarked that this was one cheque that could hardly bounce – and he cashed it.

Later, the manager of 19-year-old Miss Hannay's own bank, Lloyds at Beeston, Notts, wrote to her 'I suggest you call and collect the cheque egg against our usual form of receipt. We could not guarantee the state of the document if it were passed through the post. We are not at the moment equipped for the permanent filing of documents of this nature, but should there be a substantial increase in such drawings, no doubt the necessary equipment will be forthcoming.'

Miss Hannay, who comes from Birmingham, said last night: 'I collected the egg, but I'm afraid the bank had the last laugh. They charged me 6s. – standard charge for clearing unusual cheques, they said. Still it was worth it.'

The Sun

The Committee wish to apologize to patrons for inconvenience caused last Sunday night owing to bust mishap.

Wexford Free Press

(Gobfrey Shrdlu never *explains* anything, so in the above item we are left in a titillating state of endless speculation as to the precise nature of the mishap.)

The fire was discovered by Frances Boltz, 19, who lives with her mother, Mrs Nellie Beltz, at the 2610 address. Jacob F. Blatz, father and husband, is in the Georgetown Hospital recovering from illness.

Washington Post

Now Mr Holland followed the ordinary procedure of having tennis courts on the lawn at the back of his house, from which can be obtained a grand panoramic view towards the Chiltern Hills, which he built for himself 24 years ago.

Oxford Mail

Immediately after the ceremony the bride and bridegroom go into the vestry and sigh.

Women's magazine

New Technique Implants
Set of Debentures Direct
to Patient's Jawbone

Headline in *Niagara Falls Gazette*

*There was the chap who was asked to give up leader writing
to take a 'more responsible' position (ie paid twice as much) as
troubleshooter and puff writer for a firm of contraceptive
manufacturers.*

*He replied that although during the war he had been asked to
contribute to* La Revue des Lettres Françaises Libres, *he did not
feel competent to enter the more directly industrial side of the
business.*

UK Press Gazette

Mr Robin Page, who has threatened to start an art form that
involves stamping frogs to death, gave a demonstration of his
ideas yesterday. Wearing a silver PVC suit, silver-painted
helmet, and rubber knee-boots, he bored and pickaxed through
the concrete floor of Better Books, in Charing Cross Road.
Chips of concrete flew at the audience. After half an hour
Page struck water. Mr Robert Cobbing, the manager, then
said: 'This must stop.' Page, a leading member of the Destruction in Art Symposium, downed his shovel, sat in the hole,
and drank a bottle of beer.

He said: 'I feel very good. I have no more doubts about
anything. It is a beautiful hole. If somebody wants to buy it
the price would be £125. It's a major work, but I'm open to
offers.' Two girls in mini-skirts then paraded with placards
protesting against the possible killing of chickens. Page was
unrepentant. He said he would put frogs on a board on which
questions were written about Destruction in Art. If the
frogs gave the wrong answers they would be stamped to death.

Daily Express

Mrs Elaine Fox was told to order 250 brass taps for an
Australian Government department. She misheard and must
now explain delivery of a box of bra straps.

Tit-Bits

We can safely say that there is no repair job necessary on a car that cannot be executed more efficiently than by us.

Advert in Rhodesian paper

She looked relaxed in an attractive green, knitted Israeli dress in spite of her tight schedule.

Durban Daily News

The Bishop of - - - - who was enjoying the balmy morning driving his car, after a laborious Sunday, gave the hounds a 'view halloa' when the second fox broke, and the gallant Master rewarded his Lordship with the brush when hounds bowled him over.

Provincial paper

In the past, the Council had felt that the first thing they should do was to get the storm water out of the sewers before trying to force home-owners in. It was decided at last night's meeting that where the sewers could take the waste water without flooding, the owners should be told to get in now.

Bryan Times (Ohio)

Man Critical after Bus Backs into Him

Headline in *Middletown Press*

A friend of mine expecting some visitors to tea at her country cottage one afternoon this week, popped some scones into the oven. An hour later she was about to step into the bath when horror-stricken she remembered them. Not even stopping to grab a towel, she dashed naked downstairs into the kitchen. Her hand was on the oven handle when she heard a knock on the back door. She was panic-stricken. For she was sure her caller was the baker who, if there was no reply, would open the door and leave the bread on the kitchen table.

She darted into the nearest haven: the broom cupboard. The back door clicked open. But then, appalled, my friend heard footsteps coming across the kitchen towards the broom cupboard. The door opened. And there stood an astonished gasman. He had come to read the meter – which is in the cupboard. My friend blushed deeply – and then explained: 'I'm so sorry – I was expecting the baker ...' The gasman said 'Oh!' Then he said 'Sorry mum.' And tipping his cap politely he carefully closed the door again and walked out of the house.

Letter in *Sunday Express*

A baby sitter mixed up identical twins who had been kept in separate cots. Their parents, Captain and Mrs Douglas Wood, of Lubbock, Texas, have taken the twins back to hospital to have their footprints checked, so they can tell which is which.

Daily Express

People on a council caravan site at Bricket Wood, Herts, have been told by St Alban's Rural Council that they cannot keep cats or dogs, but a budgerigar, a parrot, or even an ostrich would be allowed. This was stated last night by the National Canine Defence League, who were arranging for a 6ft ostrich to be delivered at the site.

Daily Telegraph

His ability to drive was impaired by the drug atropine. Dr S - - -, a consultant neurologist, said the effect of having too large a nose could be to cause the recipient to screw up his eyes against the light, to roll his head from side to side, and would cause disorientation.

Nottingham Evening Post and News

BEWARE!
TO TOUCH THESE WIRES IS INSTANT DEATH
Anyone found doing so will be prosecuted

Sign on pylon

The Colonel scurried up a tree while the dog closed with the bear and killed him with four well-placed bullets.

Pennsylvania paper

Sir: for the case that your electric light should fail we beg to send you enclosed a postcard which please send us at once when you find your light out. The Company will then send you another postcard.

Yours truly,

Manager, *Siam Electricity Co Ltd*

She sat huddled in a chair, covering her ears with crossed legs.

from a short story

Brief interval to relax: The American method of ridding the countryside of dumped car wrecks – giant metal crushing and separating machines – is being imported to Britain. So when a recently appointed secretary at the Brewer's Guardian received a phone call from an agency asking for details of an advertisement run 12 months previously for a car squashing machine, she was not in the least put out. She simply left a notice for the advertisement manager asking him to follow up the inquiry.

The adman, however, was mystified. What possible connexion was there between metal crushers and brewing? None. Light dawned, and a satisfied agency received a copy of the ad it wanted – for a brewer's cask washing machine.

UK Press Gazette

WORLD water melon seed spitting contest has been granted an official charter from the Oklahoma Secretary of State. It is claimed that it will foster scientific knowledge concerning trajectory, wind resistance, and velocity that enter into the calculations of aviation and the space programme.

Daily Mail

What strange things forgetful people do to jog their memories. A friend of mine always puts his teeth in a tumbler of water and places it on the front doorstep before going to bed. This acts as a reminder to him not to leave for work without them.

Letter in *Reveille*

My wife works in the despatch department of a mail order firm. The other day a customer returned a brassière with this curt note: 'Not suitable – exchange for a pair of pillow cases.'

Letter in *Daily Mirror*

To the spiritual dangers of the moneyed life chronicled so roundly in Holy Writ is added today in *The Lancet* one telling,

My husband took an accident policy with your company, and in less than a month he was accidentally drowned. I consider it a good investment.

Testimonial in *The Finance Union*

'Good,' muttered Armand Roche to himself, hiding a smile beneath the false black beard which he always carried in his portmanteau in case of an emergency.

Women's magazine

The font so generously presented by Mrs Smith will be set in position at the East end of the Church. Babies may now be baptized at both ends.

Surrey paper

Beginning in the winter of 1938 Dr Ewing and his associates, working on the deep-sea research vessel Atlantis, began to experiment with underwear photography.

New York Times

His disappointment was keen, yet in after days he looked upon the evening as that date on which he burst from the chrysalis and became a caterpillar.

Grand Magazine

physiological footnote: in one London hospital eight cases of eye injury due to champagne corks have been treated in the past four years.

Three of the victims at the Moorfields Eye Hospital have been left with permanent defects of vision, and all, says *The Lancet*, could have been avoided by care in opening the bottles.

Significantly a search of the hospital records reveals only one other such case, in 1936. The magazine advances two theories for this: the first, the volume of champagne being drunk now as opposed to then. The number of bottles drunk in the United Kingdom rose from 2,950,291 in 1957 to 5,181,185 in 1965.

The second theory is that those natural openers of champagne bottles, the English butlers, have almost everywhere gone under the hill.

A head waiter at a London hotel where anything up to 150 champagne bottles are opened a day, told me that his 47 years in the hotel trade had yielded not a statistic. *The Lancet* says that a cork shooting from an upright bottle can reach a height of 40 ft. This means that it strikes the eye at a velocity of 45ft a second. *The Times* (by permission)

Sir, – Major C. J. L. Lewis reveals in his letter (September 16) that a country wasp, when covered with flour, will go 'zooming in a straight line' to its nest. Clearly town wasps enjoy being taken for a ride.

I caught one just now, devouring an expensive peach. I covered it, and myself, with large quantities of flour. I descended from a great height to street level and released the insect. It did not return directly to its nest. It rose vertically and vanished towards the sun. I returned to my flat.

That same white wasp was once again lunching on that same peach. How can one destroy a creature with a sense of humour?

Country wasps are just plain stupid.

Yours faithfully,
ANDREW HALL
Courtfield Road, SW7.
The Times

He had been aware from the first that she was unusually attractive; now, in her dark green dress with the low-cut, rounded neckline, he saw that she had lovely legs.

from *The Jade Venus* by G. H. Coxe

20 MILES FROM BRIGHTON
LOVELY LITTLE GENTLEMAN'S
WEEKEND RESIDENCE

Advert in *Country Life*

FOR SALE, Doctor's sailing dinghy and accessories. Doctor no further use.

Yorkshire paper

For illegal trawling and for failing to heave-to at the request of a fishery cruiser, Joseph McCarr, master of a Lossiemouth fishing boat, was fined £60 and £70 respectfully at the Sherriff Court.

Scots local paper

Easily, after a sweltering journey in a packed railway carriage, we made our way, the whole hundred thousand of us, to our appointed places.

North London paper

Sir, – I was fascinated when I read the method for finding wasps' nests. I at once tried it out, for we have many wasps here.

I caught my wasp and coated it with flour. Then I ran down the garden beneath the whitened creature. Unfortunately it soared over a ten foot wall. I was not so agile. When my bruises are healed I shall try again, but this time will use self-raising flour, on myself as well as the wasp.

Yours faithfully,

NORMAN WILLIAMS

Sydney Place, Bath.

The Times

The wife of a steelworker in Romford, Essex, complained that her husband's whiskers tickled her in bed. He was so attached to his beard, however, that he shaved off only one side, so that the cheek nearest to his wife should be smooth.

News agency story

A few years ago a Hungarian was travelling by train to Budapest. He had some bees in milk bottles with brown paper covering. Somehow the bees pierced the paper and climbed up the man's legs. To avoid being stung he explained his plight to women in the compartment, who withdrew.

He took off his trousers – and an express travelling in the opposite direction set up such a draught the trousers were whisked into the corridor. They wrapped round the neck of a ticket inspector, who was attacked by the bees. Someone pulled the communication cord, the train pulled up – and caught fire.

Officials noticed a man without trousers, and thought he was an escaped lunatic. He was arrested and strait-jacketed. It took the bee expert three days to convince asylum doctors that he was sane.

News agency story

BUFFALO SWEPT OFF
FEET BY MENDELSSOHN CHOIR

Headline in Canadian paper

It is not considered polite to tear bits off your beard and put them in your soup.

Etiquette book

Whenever eggs are cheap the fowls yield a fair supply, and when they become dear production stops.

Pall Mall Gazette

Mr Richards had two daughters, Ethel Mary and Gwendoline Florence. To the former he left an annuity of £200 so long as she remained a sprinter.

South Wales Echo

Our photograph shows Mr and Mrs H. J. Hill leaping the Hurlingham Church Hall yesterday after the marriage ceremony.

Buenos Aires Herald

TREATED LIKE DOG BY WIFE
Husband cooked for thirty years

Daily Telegraph

NOTICE

£5 REWARD. – Whereas some person or persons stabbed my Donkey on the 26th of January, and well-known about Town, and has since died through the wound inflicted. I hereby offer the above Reward to any person giving any information concerning the cruel deed.

WILLIAM CAMERON, Cape Town, 1881

Journalistic Jumbles

Madame Ivy Cannon, a charwoman employed at the Ministry of War, has been given two years' imprisonment plus a £500 fine for covering her jam-pots with top secret military documents.

Paris-Presse

Middleborough, Mass, lies 34 miles S by E from Boston, 14 miles SSW from Plymouth, and 10 SE from Taunton. Incorporated 1660. Population, 5005.

In 1763, Shubael Thompson found a land turtle, marked on the shell J.W., 1747. Thompson marked it and let it go. Elijah Clapp found it in 1773; William Shaw found it in 1775; Jonathan Soule found it in 1790, and Zenas Smith, in 1791: each marked it with his initials. Whether the *critter* is dead or gone to the west, we have no account.

Robb's Cabinet of Curiosities

A grindstone ordered from England in 1898 was delivered to the customer in Bunbury, Western Australia, in August 1962. The ship in which it was being transported had sunk sixty-four years earlier, and the grindstone had been salvaged by an underwater explorers' club.

Reveille

For nearly three-quarters of an hour the fire blazed without any real abatement, and it was only when it had burned itself out that there was any real diminution in the intensity of the flames.

Dundee Advertiser

Miss Crichton pluckily extinguished the blaze while Herr Eckold pulled the orchestra through a difficult passage.

Daily Express

It is not often a burglar comes across a house, or indeed business premises, that is properly protected with burglar proof tail canapes. The Hungarians use it in much greater quantity to give its mild flavour to goulashes and chicken dishes.

Nottinghamshire Free Press

This film stars Stewart Grainger playing a white hunter in Africa who sells his prize possessions to finance a last safari to kill Big Red, a killer elephant which has obsessed him at the Essoldo.

Blackburn Times

Girl (18) seeks post as housemaid, where lady would be willing to learn.

The Scotsman

The Court at Ballyhunis, Eire, has granted an extension of licensing hours for the Western Hotel until 1 am on October 1, when the local branch of Alcoholics Anonymous will hold their annual dinner.

Henry Fielding, *The Sun*

In 1950, legal history was made when an Australian worker won damages from his Melbourne employers because he dislocated his jaw while yawning at work. The courts decided that the damage caused by yawning was an industrial injury. Reason: the man's job was so monotonous he couldn't help yawning.

The Underwriters' Council of Melbourne agreed that in future they would pay full benefit to anyone who was injured through yawning at work.

Weekend

Found, one set false teeth to fit black cat.

Bristol Evening Post

In a letter in the *British Medical Journal*, Stephen Power of the Royal London Homeopatic Hospital recalls a case where a parson's breath caught fire every time he tried to blow out the altar candles. Cause of the fiery breath turned out to be a duodenal ulcer which led to the buildup of an inflammable gas inside the parson. After he was operated on, Power continues, 'the parson was able to carry out his duties in a more decorous fashion.'

Associated Press/Readers' Digest

Edible-snail hunters of Switzerland are to be given a 1¼ in aluminium ring. If a snail can pass through, it must be released. Infringement may mean six months' imprisonment.

Tit-Bits

Across a broad stubborn nose he carried a pair of gold-rimmed spectacles, a neat grey lounge suit, and a blue shirt with collar to match.

from a novel

Fortunately for the workman the glass fell perpendicularly, for had it fallen vertically the accident in all probability would have proved serious.

Taranaki Daily News

One of the many engagements that are always announced at the close of the season is that of Miss Caroline Stackley.

The World

FOR SALE – Cottage piano made in Berlin, owner getting grand.

Advert in The Pioneer

Slough Borough babies have their big chance at the baby show. Entries can be made on the ground and during the evening the last eight will contest the Berks and Bucks darts championship.

Windsor, Slough & Eton Express

CAIRO, Tuesday. – Cairo shopkeeper Abdel Meguid Matar was so certain he had bought an empty safe from Port Said's Israeli synagogue that he waited four years to open it.

But this week when a local locksmith produced the right key, he found the safe stuffed with gold and jewels.

Reuter

'We like not to be surprised in this business,' said the factory inspector, 'but the shop assistant who cut her *toe* off with a bacon slicer just shows you the sort of thing we are sometimes up against. She had stood on it to close a window.'

The Observer

A father is seeking insurance cover against his 16-year-old daughter losing her virginity before she marries. But he is unlikely to succeed, for in a historic ruling last night, Lloyd's of London ruled: 'Loss of virginity is a moral hazard, and so uninsurable.'

The anxious father, it would appear, is not so much worried about his daughter's purity, but about the financial burden he will have to bear if she does lose her most priceless possession. For he comes from Sicily, where there are strong views about chastity, and a non-virgin is unlikely to get married. He is now living in Bolzano, Northern Italy, but his daughter wants to go and work as a waitress in Germany. Father has agreed – on condition that she first gets 'fully comprehensive insurance'.

He went to the nearest city, Innsbruck, in Austria, and asked the largest insurance company there to carry out a medical check on his daughter and then issue a policy – premiums 27s a month – giving him £575 if the worst comes to the worst. Perplexed, the company sent the file to Lloyd's, where a spokesman said: 'This is the strangest request ever.'

The Sun

The concert held in the Good Templars' Hall was a great success ... Special thanks are due to the Vicar's daughter who laboured the whole evening at the piano, which as usual fell upon her.

South African paper

(In *Funny Ho Ho and Funny Fantastic* I drew attention to Gobfrey Shrdlu's keen visual sense, illustrated again in the above item which is one of my favourites. – D.P.)

The breathalyser has been criticized as inaccurate, but it is merely a quick screening device, and those who give a positive reaction then have either a blood or a wine test.

Belfast News Letter

I oiled up the cylinders well before cranking, and also checked over the ignition system well, including a spirited performance of 'We came from the mountains' by Bach, and the sparking plugs. What do you think causes the engine to run unevenly?

Query in motoring paper

During the past few days three bicycles have been stolen from Exeter streets. The police consider that a bicycle thief is at work.

Western Morning News

3.8.14   *From Admiralty to destroyer flotilla at sea:*

BRITISH ULTIMATUM TO GERMANY EXPIRES
AT 23.00

From Admiralty:
COMMENCE HOSTILITIES WITH GERMANY

From flotilla leader:
IMPORTANCE OF WEARING CLEAN UNDER-
CLOTHES IN ACTION IS STRESSED. THIS MAY
MAKE ALL THE DIFFERENCE BETWEEN A
CLEAN AND A SUPPURATING WOUND.

Signals at the beginning of World War I

WANTED Bone in large quantities.
For a party in Kerala over 100 tons
of dry bones are required per month
with the requirement likely to rise
to about 300 tons per month. Those
who are in a position to supply the
above quantity either in part or full
please contact the advertiser with their
lowest rates. The minimum quantity
acceptable is a wagon load on rail.
Apply Box No 1281 Care Indian Express,
Vijayawada.

Indian paper

I didn't like the colour of my woollen bed cover so I unravelled it and used the wool to knit socks. Then I exchanged
the socks for steak and chops at my butcher's.

When I asked the butcher's wife how she liked the socks she
replied: 'I don't. I have unravelled them and knitted a nice
warm bed cover.'

Letter in *Tit-Bits*

The lad was described as lazy, and when his mother asked him to go to work he threatened to smash her brains out. The case was adjourned for three weeks in order to give the lad another chance.

Manchester paper

As formerly, the ticket-holders, with their numbers, were placed in a barrel and thoroughly shaken up.

Hamilton Advertiser

We sent sixty dresses to Miss Forsythe in December, and we have just heard that she is using our gift in roofing the Mission House.

Report of Hibernian Church Missionary Society

Mr and Miss Dymock have gone for a month to Rotorua for the benefit of Mrs Dymock's health.

New Zealand Mail

Heavy rains again fell in Khartoum and vicinity last Saturday night and several lakes have been formed in various parts of the town, some of which are still navigable. Mosquitos are not allowed to breed in them, under penalty of a heavy fine.

Egyptian Mail

My father kept a guide, published at the turn of the century by the Southern Line railway, which was called 'Requisites of Tourists'. This was for travellers in England and certainly makes one dubious of the safety or reliability of a train journey. It lists such items as: 'A rather flat portmanteau which can be stowed away under a railway carriage seat and not heavier (when filled) than can be carried by the tourist in an emergency. Two flannel shirts; two pairs of flannel trousers; two pairs of easy walking shoes, not very new; strong umbrella; salt and pepper mixed; chloroform for toothache; diarrhoea mixture; cold-in-the-head mixture; flask of brandy (always have at least half a pint at hand); dust spectacles of blue glass.'

Even if British Rail aren't all that is required, they certainly seem to have improved.

Mrs C. Woodford, Eastbourne, Kent

Letter in *Sunday Mirror*

Thirty-two-years-old Siegfried Waselberger in 1957 walked upside down from Salzburg to Vienna, a distance of one hundred and seventy-three miles. He walked on his hands, covering about a mile and a half a day, and stopped every two hundred yards for rest and refreshment.

Reveille

A notification from the Commissioner of Police today said that discharge or firing of certain varieties of crackers like atom bomb and rocket which produce a disturbing noise in or near any public place, particularly within a radius of half a mile from hospitals and nursing homes, had also been prohibited.

Madras paper

Any men wishing to make any alteration in their next-of-kin must send in a notification to Orderly Room by 5 pm.

Company orders

It appears to us that Mr Dewey would have been wielding a double-edged sword in the shape of a boomerang that would have come home to plague him and beat him by a large majority.

Northampton (Mass) Hampshire Gazette

PRESIDENTIAL ADDRESS
Tremendous output of gas

Oklahoma paper

Witness was at the house at about three o'clock on the previous afternoon, and he saw Palmer through the window. He rang the bell, and the maid answered the door, but declined to open it, and told him to go to a very warm place. He had been there about four times previously but had not seen Palmer.

Southport Guardian

As I was returning from the country I met the lady, accompanied by her small dog, which was as quiet as a mouse. I wondered at this, for I had never met it before without barking.

Barmouth Advertiser

An Indian chief who is also an Opposition Member of British Columbia's legislature called yesterday for a ban on the sale of Japanese-made totem poles – 'otherwise the Indians will go into the chopstick-making business.'

The Sun

The following remarkable event occurred at Bedford [New Hampshire], on Thursday of last week. A young girl, of about 14 years of age, was assisting in the taking away of grain in the sheaf upon a scaffold on the great beams of the barn, when she accidentally fell from the scaffold, a descent of 7 or 8 feet, on to a stake of the cart which had just been unloaded. The stake entered her body, passed up the rectum, and came out on the left side near the breast, so that she was completely transfixed upon it. The stake was so attached to others by the rave of the cart as that it could not be removed until the others were broken off, when it was forced from its socket in the cart, and the girl carried out of the barn before it could be extricated from her. During all which time the girl held on by the top of the stake, which had passed through her side sufficient for her to take hold of with both hands, 6 or 7 inches at least.

A more distressing situation cannot easily be imagined. The length of the stake which passed into her body measured full 27 inches; and in circumference was 5 inches at the largest, and at least 3 inches in the smallest part of it. And what is equally remarkable, the girl is doing very well, and likely speedily to recover – and has apparently undergone less suffering than could possibly be conceived of in such a case.

Amherst (New Hampshire) Cabinet (ca 1850?)

The mother of the bride carried a bouquet of delicately tinted chrysanthemums to match her bridegroom.

Weekly Scotsman

WEDDING RECEPTION? Try our Garages, Sheds, Greenhouses, Summer Houses, Site Cabins.

Advert in *Newcastle Evening Chronicle*

ERRATUM. We regret to state we did not have the information about John Ehrlich correct. He is not an instructor, but just a fellow. Dr Wolf is not head of the botany department. There is no botany department, it's in biology. It's not Durham University, but Duke University at Durham, North Carolina.

The Cornell Countryman

There was something about that title, Old Incestors' Trading Corporation, that inspired confidence.

The American

**SILK UNDIES REPLACE
AFRICAN NOSE RINGS**

Headline in *Chicago Herald Examiner*

To keep flies from marking electric light globes, smear them with camphorated oil.

Weekly paper

Jewellers from all over the east flocked to Florida and tossed their gems in his lap. Between 1930 and 1936 Ned Green purchased more than $10,000,000 worth of jewellery, most of which was bought while he was sitting in his limousine, double parked on Miami's Flagler Street . . . Just as he acquired stamps, coins, jewels, tractors, ships, and protegées, he bought puzzles. One order he placed with Milton H. Bradley, of Springfield, Massachusetts, called for delivery of 149 pounds of jigsaw puzzles at a cost of $456.00.

He was also able to pick up, at the reduced price of only $1,700, a real bargain which might be of interest to psychologists. This was a whale's penis, fourteen feet in length. Ned had it mounted and placed on top of the balcony facing the Round Hills doorway. Only a chosen few knew what this trophy really was.

> from *The day they shook the plum tree* by
> Arthur H. Lewis (Longmans, Green, 1964).

A Michigan farmer found his baby strangled by a snake, the other day, and to make matters better he brained his wife with a hoe, and went insane.

> News item of 1869

WHAT WAKENS THE BIRDS in the morning?
They get no cups of tea or knocks on
the door. Wouldn't you like to waken with
the birds with a song in your heart,
lovely feeling, then read 'Rheumatism
and Mental Depression, etc' 4/-
post free from Peter Atkins, 7 Crossman
Street, Eastbourne.

> Advert in *Daily Telegraph*

Mr and Mrs Webster Martin are the proud parents of a 10-pound son born to little Alice and Ethel Carney who are slowly recovering from a serious case of scarlet fever.

Cambridge (Ohio) Daily Jeffersonian

The uncertain character of the weather makes it highly undesirable that the Prime Minister should venture out before his convalescence is practically complete. Many callers continue to make inquiries at 10 Downing St. Yesterday Lord L—— was among their number, pressing his throat, throwing him to the ground.

Aberdeen Free Press

Owing to a plague of wasps in the Sheffield district, farmers have had to stop harvest operations to take wasps wasp nests before they could gather in their wasps.

Edinburgh Evening Dispatch

At 18 days of age I could pick out and separate my cockerels, really a remarkable feature.

Advert in *The World*

To brighten gold braid, give it a cake, put it whole into a steamer and steam for 20 minutes; it will then be thoroughly warm. Split in two toast and butter well.

Brooklyn Daily Times

T – R staff please note: – The customer is always right – misinformed perhaps, inexact, bullheaded, fickle, ignorant, and absolutely stupid – but never wrong.

Quoted in *Removals and Storage*

WIFE AGREED TO BE HIT ON SATURDAYS

by our parliamentary staff

The new ground for divorce, that since the respondent has behaved so that the petitioner 'cannot reasonably be expected to live with the respondent', was retained in the Divorce Reform Bill yesterday by the Commons Standing Committee on the Bill without a division.

Mr Abse (Pontypool, Lab) said that a woman called on him professionally complaining about her husband. She was bruised and battered. He sent for the husband, whose solution was that he would be content to knock his wife about only on Saturday night, instead of every night.

When Mr Abse told the wife of this offer, she said: 'Saturday nights only? That will do nicely.'

The Times (by permission)

Pink elephants a publican can understand. But landlord Bill Glover suspected something fishy when one of his regulars told him: 'I've just run over a shark in your car park.'

For, apart from anything else, Bill's pub, the Spread Eagle, in Norfolk Street, Reading, is a long way from the sea. But he stopped laughing when the customer returned tugging a 5-ft dead shark.

Bill said last night: 'It must have fallen from a lorry. The police were as baffled as I was – and they were not very keen to take it as lost property. Now it seems I am stuck with the shark unless the owner comes to collect it.'

Daily Mirror

About a month ago a long red radish reached us from a reader the normal size of a carrot.

Amateur Gardening

In the current number of a golfing weekly J. H. Taylor gives a description of the early days at Westward Ho! Golf was then played in a state of nature.

Pall Mall Gazette

International all-round Game and Live Pigeon Shot offers FOR SALE a beautiful Double-barrel 16-bore HAMMER-LESS SHOTGUN both barrels are fully choked owing to acute arthritis, owner has had to give up shooting (doctor's orders).

Advert in Manchester paper

'Very clever,' interrupted Bill, who by now was sitting with his legs over the arm of his char.

Ideal Home and Gardening

Mr Williams is married and lives at ————. He has three children either directly through Peggy T—— at the YWCA, or through the 'Cheshire Observer'.

Cheshire Observer

Note to correspondent: 'Homeless.' – You have omitted to enclose your name and address. – Editor.

Jersey Evening Post

Sailor Liam Brown picked up his glass in a pub and downed a tot of rum. Then he started to eat the glass. After biting one piece off and swallowing it, he put the glass back on the bar. A barman noticed that the glass was broken. He asked what had happened to it.

Brown explained. And, as the startled barman stared, he picked up the remains of the glass and crunched off another piece. And another. And another. And another. The manager of the pub – the Kinloch Bar at Campbelltown, Argyllshire – was called. He asked Brown to pay for the glass. Brown refused. The manager asked Brown to leave the bar. Brown threw beer over him.

Then the police arrived. They took Brown to a police station and called a doctor to examine him. 'The officers were apprehensive as to the effect the accused's diet might have on him,' Mr A. I. B. Stewart, prosecuting, told a court in Campbelltown yesterday. When the police and the doctor went to Brown's cell, they found that he had put his fist through a window and cut his arm. The glass-eating, however, had no ill-effects, said Mr Stewart.

Brown, who serves in HMS Grafton, was fined £10 – for breaking the police window.

Daily Mirror

A haggis weighing 11 lb 3 oz was eaten in 65 seconds on Waterloo station on Monday, establishing a record speed for the daily haggis-eating competition being held there during Scottish Holiday Fortnight.

The competition is to see who can gobble up a haggis fastest. The winner of the final on July 14 gets a holiday for two in Scotland. Sixty pounds of hot haggis have already been consumed.

The Times

Whether the shell of an egg is white or brown depends solely on the breed of the bird. Generally speaking a brown hen will lay a brown egg and vice versa.

Cheadle and Tean Times

Two more reports have been received of the orange ball seen in the sky on Friday night. Mrs E. M. Jones of Hill-street, described as crescent shaped, or rather like a bent red hot poker . . .

Wolverhampton *Express and Star*

A few will be seated in front of the quartet in approximately a conventional concert position, while the others will have more unusual relationships with the performers.

Western Morning News

At about one o'clock when the eclipse was on the sun, I saw a most beautiful star shining very bright, and I pointed this out to three ladies who were watching the eclipse in a bath of water. Is this an unusual occurrence?

Letter in West London paper

'Mr Perkins might be able to help you,' she said, as she took down a dusty lodger from the shelf.

Weekly magazine serial

One pound of home-made lemon curd to the owner of mounted Astronomical telescope willing to allow a couple to look at the night sky for half an hour one evening only. Please telephone Epping 0000.

Card in newsagent's window

The misfortune of a German called Helmut Winter was that he lived near two airfields used by Luftwaffe Starfighter jets. They flew so low that their airstream shook the bushes in his garden. Their noise was so loud and continuous that, on the rare occasion when there was silence, Mr Winter rushed out of his Munich home to find out what was wrong.

That, anyway, was how things used to be, until the ingenious Mr Winter fought back with his catapult. It is a formidable weapon, based on a design by the Renaissance engineer and artist Leonardo da Vinci, and constructed by a carpenter friend of Mr Winter. It was a kind of ultimate deterrent of the Middle Ages, an early example of a ballistic missile launcher.

Mr Winter's missiles were dumplings made by his wife Elisabeth. The launcher takes two at a time and it is accurate up to a range of 90ft. After enduring a three-day 129-dumpling barrage against low-flying aircraft, the Luftwaffe capitulated. An officer and three pilots from nearby Fuerstenfeldbruck air base called on Mr Winter to discuss peace terms. Said Mr Winter: 'They were worried about all the adverse publicity I was causing the Luftwaffe. They promised that in future their jets will not fly below the regulation 900 ft.'

Daily Express

A man who wanted to sue his barrister for professional negligence was refused a legal aid certificate. Later he was granted legal aid to appeal against the decision to refuse him legal aid.

The Sun

```
WANTED. — A domesticated lady to
live with an elderly lady to hell
with the cooking and housework.
```

         Notice in Agency window

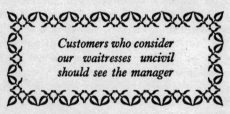

*Customers who consider
our waitresses uncivil
should see the manager*

           Notice in café

The bride wore a gown of white satin featuring scooped neckline, elbow-length sleeves, and bell-shaped skirt, with a square train a few loose slates, and the ridge tiles silk veil fell from a satin head-band.

           Southport Visitor

When a recipe includes spice, essence, in dressmaking, unsightly ridges may be formed.

           Long Eaton Advertiser

The chairman of the Passenger Transport Committee, told last night's meeting of the Plymouth City Council that he had no intention of altering the 17a bus route. 'But this does not mean we will not,' he warned.

           Western Evening Herald

HMS Brighton, the anti-submarine frigate which has been visiting the town after which she is named, claims a naval record in that during recent operations in the Red Sea an officer fried an egg on her deck by the sun's heat in four minutes. What made the achievement notable, according to the egg-frier, was that the cooking fat used for the operation was put down on the deck cold. While at Brighton there was apparently little chance of giving a repeat performance.

The Times

FILM COMPANY secretary Susan Ornstein was shaken when her mini car demolished a traffic bollard in London's Hyde Park. But not half as shaken as she was when she got the bill for putting it back up yesterday. The total: £118 5s.

Susan, 23-year-old secretary to film producer John Gilbert, said: 'I shall have to pay by instalments. And the best part of it is that the bollard has already been knocked down again.' The bill from the Ministry of Public Building and Works was carefully detailed. It read: —

Hyde Park sub carriage road repairs to Rutland Gate bollard. Two labourers, twelve hours each; one bricklayer, four hours; one bricklayer's mate, four hours; one painter, two hours; one electrician, four hours; one electrician's mate, four hours; one fitter, seven hours; one fitter's mate, seven hours. Total labour charge: £52 18s 5d.

Materials: One new cast-iron bollard post, one new octagonal lantern, two 30 volt 60 watt lamps, one bushel sand, 14 lb of cement, one quart of paint. Total materials: £66 5s 9d. Total charge £119 4s 2d. Deduct scrap value of one bollard 19s 2d. Total £118 5s.

The mini car? That was written off too.

National newspaper

GARDENS DUG, widows washed, and chimneys swept, in Tallaght area.

Advert in Dublin *Evening Herald*

These are busy days for Mr Brian Smith, landlord of the Dog and Duck. Customers often follow Mr Smith out to the magpies' cage in an outbuilding, where he fills their eager beaks with milk and small pieces of bread and meat.

Leicester Mercury

It is estimated that a quarter of a million sterling's worth of damage was done in the Butler's Gridge Wharf fire. The firemen are still playing horses on the smouldering debris.

Malta paper

At Woodford people were pouring out of buses into Epping Forest, looking green and lovely.

Evening Standard

They were all delighted to have Miss Benson back amongst them. Their best wishes would go with her next week when she set out for her holiday, and they all hoped she would return with

MEASLES AND WHOOPING-COUGH

Scottish paper

Mr Edward Clinton – The death of Mr Edward Clinton, aged 74, has occurred at his home, 1 Pillar Lane, Alresford. He leaves a widow and two sons. Cremation followed a service at Stoneham. There was a 'sing-song' in which friends and patients joined, accompanied by the Hospital Percussion Band. The chairman, Mr C. H. Jenkins, thanked all who had made the occasion an enjoyable one.

Chichester Observer

Gravediggers had started shovelling earth onto Roberto Rodriguez's coffin in the churchyard at Pecaya, Venezuela, when the lid burst open. Out scrambled Roberto protesting at the incompetence of the doctor who had certified his death and so nearly had him buried alive. Roberto's mother-in-law, standing by the graveside, collapsed and died. After doctors had made absolutely sure she was dead, she was buried in the grave so recently vacated.

Reveille

The latest novelty from Germany is a musical bed which receives the weary body and immediately 'laps it in Elysium'. It is an invention of a mechanic in Bohemia, and so constructed that by means of a hidden mechanism, pressure upon the bed causes a soft and gentle air of Auber to be played which continues long enough to lull the most wakeful to sleep. At the head is a clock, the hand of which being placed at the hour the sleeper wishes to rise, when the time arrives, the bed plays a march of Spontoni, with drums and cymbals, and in short with noise enough to rouse the seven sleepers. This unique bed becomes therefore the *ne plus ultra*, for the wakeful as well as the sluggish.

Boston Cultivator, 1846

Gladness, health, and happiness you will find, when you will travel and stay in the province of Luxembourg. The kindness of its people and its gentlemanlike hotellists will enjoy you.

Travel leaflet

Apart from her husband, a marine engineer, she was the only woman among 52 men on the trip.

Daily Express

F—— M——. Congratulations and best wishes to my daring fiancée on her 21st Birthday.

Jewish Telegraph

In addition to the usual prizes, over 50 swimming certificates were presented. The school choir sank during the evening.

Oldham Chronicle

Here the party was greeted by Mr Stilgoe, City Water Engineer, and his assistant, Mr Davies, and then driven to the replica of Liverpool Castle which was erected by the late Lord Leverhulme. Photographs of the ruins were taken, including those in the party.

Merseyside Civic Society circular

A fisherman lost his false teeth in eighty feet of water in a lake at Arkansas, USA. A week later he caught a twenty-pound catfish which he delivered to the local market. When he returned the next day he heard that some false teeth had been recovered from it. He saw at once that they were his own, and started wearing them again.

Reveille

WHEN THE SECRETARY of a California flying club received a letter from women members of a nearby nudist camp complaining that they had been buzzed by low-flying aircraft, he responded immediately by placing a notice in the club bar. It read: 'Pilots are reminded that on no account should they fly low over the ladies in the nudist camp located 14 miles from here on a course of 244 degrees true.'

Evening Standard

Here lies the body of JEEMS HUMBRICK
who was accidentally shot
on the banks of the Pacus river
by a young man.

He was accidentally shot with one of the large Colt's revolver with no stopper for the cock on it was of the old-fashioned kind brass mounted and of such is the Kingdom of Heaven.

An epitaph in a San Diego churchyard

In the Nuts (unground) (other than groundnuts) Order, the expression nuts will have relevance to such nuts other than groundnuts as would but for this amending order not qualify as nuts (unground) (other than groundnuts) by reason of their being nuts (unground).

from a government publication

A houseowner in Golders Green was forced to leave his house through dangerous cracks in the walls.

Hendon paper

As he uttered the all-important word he dropped his voice, but she just managed to catch it.

Short story in evening paper

The service was conducted by the Rev Charles Harris MA, the bridegroom. The wedding was of a quiet nature owing to the recent death of the bride.

Blackpool Times

Unfurnished sc flat, 2 bedrooms, urgently required at moderate rent by Customs Officer and wife expecting quiet baby.

Advert in *Wallasey News*

If they could save children from dying before the age of one there was a better prospect of them reaching to adolescence.

South London paper

The door opened and Keith stood there. For a brief moment they looked at each other and then she ran into his rams.

Personality (South Africa)

HOTEL THE GRANDY

No 2 Bonny Street, Port Harcourt

- -

(formerly and famously known as METROPOLE)

THIS IS WHERE GENTS HAVE THEIR REST

YOU REALLY NEED REST:— *All works and no rest makes
James a dull Boy.*

HOTEL THE GRANDY SERVES THE PURPOSE

*Well designed for respectable gents.
All kinds of diet available.
Drinks in exhaustible.
Service by fancy boys and girls.
Very attractive and captivating
Sleeping accommodation well reserved.*

A VISIT IS ENOUGH FOR ALL YOU NEED

FIRST FLOOR:— Roasted Chickens, Salad, Fry Fish, Meat-
Rolls, Sanguages etc.

SECOND FLOOR:— Pure English diet.

WHY NOT ENJOY YOURSELF WITH OTHERS

Phone No 442 PH   Mrs M. E. Jane
Managing Proprietress

Hotel leaflet

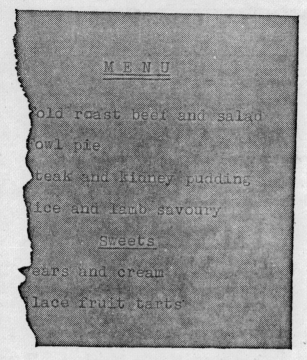

MENU

old roast beef and salad

owl pie

teak and kidney pudding

ice and lamb savoury

Sweets

ears and cream

lace fruit tarts

Menu found in 'The Fig and Fishbone' teashop

The verger reports that two blue book-makers were left in the Lady Chapel on Easter Eve.

Parish Magazine

At the Lincoln County picnic at Vineland, Ontario, the rolling pin throwing contest was won by Mrs W. H. Upsall, who threw the rolling-pin 67 feet. Mr Upsall won the 100 yards dash for married men.

Canadian paper

Generations of parents have warned their rebellious off-spring: 'If you don't wash your ears you'll start growing pot-atoes in them.' And that is what almost happened to one small boy in Connecticut, America. A bean found its way into his ear . . . and began to grow. It had sprouted a half-inch shoot when it was removed – four months after it had taken root.

Weekend

	Pronounced as
This railroad is remarkable for the number of bridges, viaducts, cuttings, and embankments; the great tunnel is a wonderful piece of workmanship.	Dis reil'-rou izz ri-mark'-abl for de nâm-bâr óv bridjz, vai'á-dâkts, kât'tings, énnd embenk'mêntss; de greit tânnel izz â uânn'dâr-ful piss óv uârk'mênnxip.
This is a line with a double way.	Diss izz â láinn uid â dâb'-bl' uei.
This rapidity causes me some uneasiness; the train has rendered the rails very slippery.	Diss râpid'-i-ti kózz's mi sâmm ânn-i-zi-ness; de treinn hézz rênn'-dârd de reilz vér'i slip'-par-i.
You have nothing to fear; the engine is sufficiently powerful and no accident has ever happened here.	Iu hév nâ'-cing tu fi'-ar; de ennd'-djinn izz sâffish'-ent-li páu'-âr-ful énd nou ék'ci-dênt héz év'âr hép'--p'nd hi'âr.
Now we have arrived. Look at the crowd of porters waiting to seize our luggage.	Nau ui hév ar-ráiv'd. Luk at de kraud óv pór'-târz uei'-ting tu sizz au'-âr lâg'-eidj.

from an English phrase-book for Portuguese tourists

FOOT TROUBLES RELIEVED
Custom made arches designed and
made for your particular
discomfort

Advert in *Los Angeles Times*

We cannot be held responsible for the inefficacy of the stuff unless our label appears on it.

Ceylon store leaflet

Yesterday in this column the wording appeared: 'fellows in the back row, among whom I was with'. That was a typographical error. It was originally written: 'fellows in the back row, among whom I was which'.

We trust that makes everything clear.

San Francisco Chronicle

MATRESSES REMADE
PILLOWS CLEANED
New ticks supplied at reasonable prices.

Advert in *Yorkshire Post*

Mrs Jenning brought up the question of providing kneelers for the College pews in the North Aisle; after discussion it was resolved to leave the matter in the hands of the Standing Committee.

Kent parish magazine

Extraordinary Hailstone. The Hartford Mirror says that a hailstone, or rather mass of ice fell during a thunderstorm, in the presence of several persons, in Monson, Mass, of the following very extraordinary dimensions: Extremes 4 ft long, 3 ft wide, 2 ft thick. The appearance is said to have been that of a compact body of hail stones, as firmly united as hail usually is. After removing the rough parts of the body there remained a solid block 2 feet 3 inches long, 1 foot 6 inches wide, and 1 foot 3 inches thick.

New England Farmer, 1823

One guest at a wedding on the Riviera was not recognized by the groom although he introduced himself as Cousin Jules. He was turned over to the police, whose investigations revealed that the man had lived for several years by attending weddings, christenings, and funerals to get free meals, always saying he was Cousin Jules when anyone questioned him. The police found there was no charge which fitted his offences and discharged him.

Reveille

The 25 butchers of Scunthorpe, Lincolnshire, yesterday beat the world record set up by the banger-loving burghers of Konigsberg, Germany, in 1701. Last night the weights and measures inspector solemnly measured the Great Sausage of Scunthorpe – all 3,010 ft of it.

Butchers and the Fatstock Marketing Corporation gave the meat free and today the sausage will be made into links and sold for the mayor's appeal fund. Main problem was joining the skins together. The average skin is 50 ft. They had to join 60 skins to hold the Scunthorpe sausage. The butchers mixed six and a half hundredweight of pork with one and a half hundredweight of cereal and seasoning.

Daily Mail

VOLUNTARY WORKERS PUT IN CHURCH HEATING PLANT

The Barnet Press

The courts have held that in the case of an auto driver who neglects the utmost precaution at a railway crossing and is struck by a train, he is guilty of negligence and not entitled to recover.

Herrington (Kansas) *Sun*

Death was due to strangulation due to asphyxiation caused by strangulation resulting from gagging.

Evening News

Pickles, who was fined twice, ran a big risk of losing his licence but there were exterminating circumstances in one case.

Lancs paper

Giving evidence, Mr Mayes said that he had been in the licensed trade for 46 years and that was the worst incident he had had in his experience, including 22 years in Sheffield.

High Peak News

New York, Thursday. The body of Dr James Bedford, a retired professor who died of lung cancer, is to be kept frozen in liquid nitrogen in response to his own hope that he might be restored to life when a cure is found. He left £1,420 to the Cryonics Society of Southern California for the experiment.

Three scientists began the freezing process before Dr Bedford died just over a week ago, at the age of 73. Artificial respiration and external heart massage were applied to try to keep the brain alive while he was frozen for eight hours in an envelope of ice. Today the body arrived in Phoenix, Arizona, where it will be preserved frozen in a capsule of liquid nitrogen. No process has yet been discovered for restoring life after it is extinct.

Daily Telegraph

John Beaumont is looking for a bride with something extra special. He wants to marry a redhead, aged about 40 . . . and she must have 4,500 cigarette coupons. John is advertising for a wife in a weekly newspaper.

'I've already got 4,500 coupons,' John explained yesterday. 'With twice that number we could have a really nice wedding present.' What if he had an offer of marriage from a pretty girl with no coupons? The answer, says John, who earns £20 a week, will be 'No'.

Daily Mirror

SQUATTER BENDS THE CHURCH ORGAN

A squatter in the church organ struck a discordant note – and caused about £500 worth of damage. The irreverent intruder made a makeshift bed among the organ pipes in rafters at St Margaret's Church, Portsmouth. And he made room for relaxation by bending several of the pipes out of line.

Daily Mirror

LADIES MAY HAVE FITS UPSTAIRS

Shanghai tailor's sign

The early Britons made their houses of mud and there was rough mating on the floors.

Exam answer

MILKMAN
No milk today, by today I
mean tomorrow, as I wrote
this yesterday.

Note to milkman

GIRL WITH A DETECTIVE IN HER BOOT

Headline in *Daily Mirror*

My bungalow used to be in a private and secluded position until a developer erected some houses nearby. The lounge window of the house nearest mine is exactly four feet away from my bathroom window which is not frosted.

As a woman I find this most embarrassing. When I stand up in my bath, I can be seen by all and sundry. I do hope the valuation officer will come and see for himself.

Letter to valuation panel

Three magistrates had to decide yesterday which would dry out first – a man or a car. The man ALFRED R – – – –, 56, motor inspector, of Beech Road, Southgate, was found sitting in his brand-new car in the Thames at Isleworth by a constable, who adjudged him to be 'unsteady and quite drunk'.

R– – – – was accused at Brentford of being in charge of a car while unfit through drink. He said he parked his car near the river before going out drinking. When he returned the tide had come in and flooded it. 'I was so sick at seeing it in the river, I just sat in it,' he added. The constable who arrested him said: 'The car was so waterlogged it would have been impossible for him to have driven it.'

Mr V. C. DENTON, the chairman, said: 'We must decide whether the man would have sobered up before the car dried out.' Fining R– – – – £20 he said there was some doubt whether the car would have dried out before R– – – – would have sobered up.

Daily Telegraph

From the funeral director's point of view, undertaking is a service industry: the raw material is supplied by the customer, processed according to the customer's order, and returned to the customer in finished form.

Cambridge Journal quoted in *New Statesman*'s
'This England' column

Do not quarrel with an angry person, but give him a soft answer. It is commanded by Holy Writ, and furthermore, it makes him madder than anything else you could say.

Sanderstead Church News

AT LAST

A WARM TOILET SEAT. LIKE SITTING ON TOAST

FITS TO MOST EXISTING SEATS

NO RUNNING COSTS

One minute fixing   Pat. Pend.

ONLY 7/6 + 2/- P. + P.

& CO. LTD.

BIRMINGHAM 19

Advert in Tit-Bits

'Here's Miller running in to bowl. He's got two short legs and one behind.'

BBC commentator

'I am afraid this scheme is a sacred cow which has come home to roost with a vengeance, and a great bang.'

Tory MP in House of Commons

DEMAND FOR GOD ON PARIS
BULLION MARKET TODAY DROPPED
TO ITS LOWEST LEVEL FOR OVER A
MONTH

Reuter

AMAZING OFFER. Fish and chip fryer, made from chip-resistant enamel.

Advert on cigarette coupon

On May 6, B——— called at his house and, brandishing a chopper, used abusive language. 'I told him not to do that on a Sunday,' went on A———. At 5 am on May 8, A——— alleged, B——— walked into his bedroom and hit him 12 times on the head with a chopper. Afterwards they took a cup of tea together in the bedroom.

News of the World

A talk by Sir A. G———, originally entitled 'The Maintenance of Noble Standards in Music as an Inspiration for Nobler Lives', took a somewhat different course, chiefly owing to the lecturer's obviously sincere desire to impress upon his hearers the necessity for combating the Communist menace.

Musical Times quoted in *New Statesman*

News today of the ultimate in *graffiti* from the gentlemen's lavatory of a 17th century pub in Chester. It was discovered when the landlord of the Bear and Billet in Lower Bridge Street decided to have the old loo demolished.

On the back of the ancient slate slabs that formed an essential part of the convenience they found in ornate gilded script the Lord's Prayer, a chunk of Genesis, and the Ten Commandments.

The Sun

At the Cattle Show in Rhode Island, Dr Benj Dyer of Providence, appeared clad in a complete suit of silk, of a superior quality, manufactured in his own family, even from the culture of the trees to the growing of the worms, producing the material.

The Providence Journal, 1823

On Friday and Saturday of the stampede, the two bathtubs in the basement of the First National Bank Building will be open for use.

Hinsdale (Montana) *Tribune*

Dr Grace Simmerhahn has returned from New York where she was killed on account of the illness of her brother.

Clinton (Iowa) *Herald*

Cut about $\frac{1}{2}$ loaf of French bread into thin slices and dry out in oven. Pour soap into earthenware casserole, put bread on top, sprinkle with $\frac{1}{2}$ cup grated cheese and set in oven long enough to brown the cheese.

Pittsburgh Sun Telegraph

Owing to the fuel crisis officials are advised to take advantage of their typists between the hours of 12 and 2.

Notice in Town Hall

During the remainder of the stay of the Goodwill Mission from America there will be extra patrols out in the West End to see that there is no further trouble.

Report in London paper

The hostel will subsequently be adapted for the usual two sex function and will then accommodate about forty people.

Circular on Lakeland Youth Hostels

Dr Harry W. Boothe, 44, told a vets' conference in Chicago that he frequently had to 'dry out' drunken dogs. It was easier than getting humans off drink, he said, because basically dogs are not voluntary drinkers – 'somebody helped them get hooked'.

He said the treatment was to give the animals injections and sympathy. 'Two boxers were chronic cases. I discovered that one was following the other downhill. One was a bar dog in a joint where the girls were emptying drinks they had persuaded customers to order into a bucket behind a curtain. The boxer was lapping it up and became an almost incurable alcoholic.

'There was a poodle who drank with his master and was always hung over and in need of drying out. But he would always go back on the stuff again. And a Yorkshire terrier with a great thirst weighed only about six or seven pounds and would drink his weight in booze. He used to roll over and was always coming in for treatment. The drying-out treatment lasts about three or four days and costs between £15 and £20, including dog hospital care.'

Daily Mirror

Mohammed Murad was rushed with police escort to Cairo's racecourse where bets were placed on his behalf. But thousands of racegoers were shocked and complained about Mohammed's presence. For when he was set down, tenderly, in the 2s stand, he was in his coffin. He had died the day before.

Now Egypt's Ministry of the Interior have held inquiries into why the coffin was diverted from its course to the cemetery. The four escorting policemen have said that they suddenly felt an irresistible power from inside the coffin, forcing them to take it to the racecourse. There, they felt impelled to bet on certain horses which the deceased would have backed. And, by some divine guidance, these horses won.

The People

Edinburgh's Director of Education, referring to sex education, is reported to have said: 'Teachers noticed a new look in children's eyes after an experimental course.'

Letter in Sunday Express

The —— Branch of Old Age Pensioners met on Thursday and listened with interest to Dr Thomas. Several members are still ill.

Cardiff and Suburban News

Haynes might easily have killed his nephew and people had got to learn that the use of knives, even on relatives, would not be tolerated.

Richmond and Twickenham Times

Miss Goldhurst, has NO Male Goat this season, and refers all clients to Mr Harris.

Advert in Grantham Journal

The Coroner warned the mother: 'Whether you think a child is dead or not, don't place it under a bucket in the garden in future.'

Hastings and St Leonards Observer

Granting a decree to a wife at Swansea Assizes, Mr Commissioner O. Temple-Morris said her husband wrote her a letter which should not have been sent to a dog.

News of the World

GRAVEDIGGERS are being timed under a work study scheme organized by the council at Yeovil, Somerset, who will pay the men more 'if they increase output'.

The Sun

'Alan broke his leg in two places a month ago at nursery school – we don't know how,' his father laughed.

Slough Observer

Push-Button Door Locks

EUREKA type new SEGNAL

the most complete practical rational locks for the doors of the Hotel Rooms
BY THEM

THE CLIENT, locking up the door, automatically releases the RED and advertises outside that he is in his room and NO TROUBLING

WHEN THE CLIENT FORGETS TO LOCK UP, the inside signaller remains WHITE and so in each moment it advertises him of the forgetfulness.

THE RED SIGNALLER has so the function of the THIRD LOCKING, giving to the Client the SECURITY TO BE NOT TROUBLED, without the inconvenience the Client be obliged to rise from the bed or to come out of the bath for opening to the called waitress.

WHEN THE CLIENT LOCKS UP FROM OUTSIDE, the signaller returns or remains WHITE, advertising the waitress that the room is WIDE.

Leaflet with lock

WANTED – Man to clean pig's feet; piece-work.

Advert in Liverpool Echo

Lie flat on the back, with the feet tucked under the wardrobe. Keep the hands at the sides and raise the legs until they are vertical. Very slowly lower again.

South African paper

Usually the annual effort is a sale of work and a concert, but this year so as not to put too great a strain on supporters, a concert and a sale of work have been arranged.

Exeter Express and Echo

The leather bag in which he made daily trips to New York with money and papers was fastened to his shoulders like a knapsack.

New York Herald Tribune

He stopped and re-lit his cigarette with a great light in his eyes.

Scottish paper

Among those present, with whom his Lordship shook hands very cordially were three men, one armless.

Daily Mail

For sanitation purposes
please sanit in the pots provided
and not on the floor.

Sign in Ladies' Room in Chinese
restaurant in India

The unemployment rate among the spiders of Strensall
Common, near York, which have long been known for their
hard work and precise craftsmanship, is showing a steady increase, directly attributable to the advance of modern tech-
nology in the theodolite-making industry.

Thirty years ago the female spider of the species Epeira
diademata, easily distinguished by the white cross upon its
back, was the main source of supply for the cross lines used
for sighting in theodolites made by Vickers Instruments
Limited at York.

Every autumn a junior apprentice would be sent the four
miles from the factory to the common to collect the insects.
Some years he returned with 50 or 60. Now, though the
journey is still made, the gossamer needed every year could be
spun by only three spiders. When the older models of theodo-
lite are discontinued, the spiders may be redundant.

The invention which is putting the spiders out of work,
said the works manager of the factory, Mr Eric Cussans, is a
process of vacuum depositing of metal upon glass, which
produces a line even finer than the three ten thousandths of
an inch that is the width of a spider's thread.

'You put the spider on to a pencil end or a stick,' said Mr
Cussans, 'and give it a tap with your index finger so that it
falls. Then we take metal forks with two prongs about four
inches long and wrap the web around them. We get about three
or four feet a fork and about 40 ft from a spider, though they
sometimes give up to 100 ft.'

The Guardian

Between lunch and dinner take another tumbler of cold water. Take a glass of cold water half an hour after lunch, half an hour after tea, and before going to bed at night. Never drink between meals.

Woman's Life

Mr James Higgins of USA spoke next. His was also an extremely humorous address, full of amusing antidotes.

West Indian paper

Thomas Lynch was fined $4 and costs at a Chicago Police Court for biting a dog in the course of an argument. Lynch admitted that the dog was a stranger to him.

Scots paper

Our Brussels correspondent reports that Belgium intends to remain outside the Anglo-British controversy.

Daily paper

At Otley yesterday William Sainsbury was fined 20s and £3 6s costs for driving a motorcar to the danger of the public; Herbert Franks was fined 40s for a similar offence; and George Morris was paid 20s for driving a motorcar negligently.

Yorkshire paper

AMERICAN car dealer Gordon Butler – who will take *anything* as a trade-in – recently accepted an elephant as a £1,071 down-payment on a new car.

An animal trainer from California walked into Butler's showroom at Worcester, Massachusetts, and offered to trade-in one of the three elephants he had with him in a trailer for a new car. After a phone call to find the value of an elephant, Butler let the animal trainer have the car.

Weekend

Six bulls were killed on a farm near Pinerolo, Italy, yesterday . . . by a snail. The snail shorted a wire to an electric well pump as the bulls drank from a nearby trough. They were electrocuted.

Daily Mirror

SCOTS STICKY ON FOOD VANS

Headline in *Motor Transport*

'That's nothing,' sniffed Palermo house-painter Lorenzo Guarnieri on reading about a Spanish waiter who has 24 fingers and toes. 'I have 26.'

'In our family we never thought anything of it. But if they make such a fuss about someone who only has 24 fingers and toes what would they say about us (his mother, sister, and himself) who have 78 between us.' Guarnieri, aged 25, his mother Rosalia, 56, and sister Antonina, 26, all have six fingers on each hand and seven toes on each foot. They say they never have trouble with shoes, but have to have gloves made specially.

Reuter

The century-old 24-hour clock is built into the wall of the old Greenwich Observatory, now Largelyha Museum.

Japan Times

Room and Bedroom to forigen caple or dzentelmens near sea baths. Electerik bels hot voter and seperet salon.

Brazilian paper

Three girls gained State Scholarships which took them to B—— College, and at 2s per lb are of excellent quality.

Essex paper

My husband keeps telling me to go to hell. Have I a legal right to take the children?

Letter to Dorothy Dix

Friday September 6, the Rt Hon J. Enoch Powell at Birmingham Press Club Dinner, Birmingham Press Club. (Not open to the Press.)

Handout from Conservative Central Office

Palace's defence was suspect during quick breakaways and a poor back pass from Blyth brought Jackson out of his area to kick off Treacy's toes.

Evening News

An unappreciative employer forces sluggish and immature man, nearly 33, to find almost any job in the lovely Lake District; over-payment for unimpressive talents might conjure up a flicker of interest in the toils of business, whilst a longing for an 'away from it all' existence – if fulfilled – could result in early senility; single, of course. Replies, if any, to Box 504.

Kendall Gazette

SUBMARINE IN BATTLE WITH SWORDFISH

An American midget submarine has had an underwater fight to the death with a swordfish. It happened off the coast of Georgia, when the submarine, from the research ship Lulu, dived to explore the ocean. The swordfish, basking in the warm waters of the Gulf Stream, resented the interloper on its territory. It attacked.

The fight ended when the fish's sword became jammed in the hull of the submarine. The submarine was scratched. The sword was kept as a trophy.

And the fish? It was eaten.

Reuter / Daily Mirror

Since her fiancé had a habit of declaiming poetry, the young woman driver was not perturbed when, as she took a blind corner fast, he exclaimed in alarm: 'Brake, brake, brake!'

'Even I know *that* one – "on thy cold gray stones, O Sea!",' she chirped, two seconds before hitting the back of a coal cart.

Peterborough in *Daily Telegraph*

Men compromise only 1.5 per cent of the South's nursing students.

The Atlanta Journal

They thought she was 99 but are now convinced she is a centurion.

Leicester Evening Mail

Son of a well-known London impressario, he was born at Dolgelly, North Wales, when only a toddler.

Bognor Regis Post

Midfield play became erotic.

Leicester Sports Green 'Un

The route taken by the Queen was lined by clapping, cheering crows.

Leicester Evening Mail

'The first my client knew of the accident was when it occurred.'

Solicitor in magistrates' court

In a row of beds in Weymouth, Dorset, Hospital, are four children — ALL from one family, ALL admitted within six days, and ALL with appendicitis.

First came six-year-old Peggy Woodward, desperately ill and now recovering; then Victor, seven, Peggy's twin sister Jean, and Robert, twelve, admitted yesterday.

Sunday Express

Two of the 124 competitors in the Derbyshire Amateur and Professional Golfers Alliance's four-ball competition at Allestree Park yesterday died on the course. Station Officer Cecil Mart, aged 42, of Lexington Road, Spondon, Derby, due to retire from the Derby Borough Fire Brigade shortly because of thrombosis, collapsed on the fourth tee. An hour later Mr Kenneth Knighton, aged 45, a bank under-manager, of Allestree, Derby, died at the 11th hole. The competition was cancelled.

Daily Express

When two motorists involved in an accident at Wetwang, near Driffield, Yorkshire, came to exchange names they refused to believe each other, for Mr Cyril White had been in collision with Mr Cyril White. The two Mr Whites live 60 miles apart — one at Leeds and the other at Wetwang. Their meeting in the fog resulted in damage to the cars but no personal injuries.

The Times

Sir, — My brother, the late Adml Sir James Ferguson, was second in command of the big guns of the Naval Division on the Paardeburg side in the South African War. The names of the captains of his two guns were Mr Cannon and Mr Ball.

Susan G. Baird, Edinburgh.

Letter in *Sunday Times*

'Spofford' starring Melvyn Douglas will close after its Sunday matinee on June 9 at the ANTA theatre. The play will have had a run of 203 performances. The loss will amount to $125,000, according to a spokesman, Herman Shumlin, who adapted the comedy from Peter De Vries' navel.

New York Times

MAN STOWS AWAY TO SEE GIRL FRIED

Bristol Evening Post

The Roman Catholics obtained a firm footing in Central Africa, and sent forth several missionaries into the equatorial regions. They were accustomed to begin their work by buying heathen children and educating them. The easiest and best way to prepare them is first to wipe them with a clean towel; then place them in dripping-pans and bake them until they are tender. Then you will have no difficulty in rubbing them through a sieve, and will save them by not being obliged to cut them in slices and cook for several hours.

Montreal paper

'I am brokenhearted because my daughter wants to marry a boy who is not of our religion, who hasn't a job or a penny to his name. How can I stop her from marrying him, and on which side does the bride's mother sit?'

Letter to Dorothy Dix

When Larry and Kitty Coulson went fishing on the Norfolk Broads, Kitty's only catch was an old shoe. She took it home to Romford, Essex, as a souvenir. Jokingly, Larry put it in a glass case – and there it stayed until Kitty's sister spotted it and gasped: 'My shoe!'

She backed up her claim by producing the other one to the pair. She had lost a shoe during a holiday on the Broads six weeks earlier.

Tit-Bits

FALSE TEETH FOR COWS

A DENTIST says he knows what it takes to produce a contented cow ... false teeth. Dr Nelson Cruz Arias has fitted out a number of cows with dentures – with 'satisfying' results. He said: 'Cow dentistry is going to be very much a thing of the future. I anticipate being a very busy man.'

Weekend

Quite a number of killings, burnings, and robberies occurred during the holidays. One fellow killed his brother, for a Christmas trick.

Dahlonega (Georgia) *Nugget*

He did not loose her lips now but held them between his. She felt great thrilling waves running over her. His hands groped over her body – every touch made tremors run over her as she lay in his arms. And she was kissing him, kissing him on the neck – there were deep, mumbling sounds in his throat. He was laughing, a laugh deep down inside.

from a magazine story

In court he pleaded guilty to having an offensive weapon and pleaded not guilty to using insulting stomach of another man in the behaviour.

Yorkshire Evening Post

At the end of the two-hour itinerary, refreshments were provided by Ready-Mix Concrete Ltd.

Eastwood and Kimberley Advertiser

No authenticated case has been known in which sterile parents have transmitted that quality to their offspring.

Letter to *The Times*

The Countess of —— who was with a merry party wore nothing to indicate that she was a holder of four Scottish titles.

Scottish paper

COW SAVES A LIFE

Hauls farmer by tail from blazing building

Sussex paper

'We saw 26 deer come down to feed,' sighed Helen Bowman, and added that they were wearing warm sweaters at the time.

Miami Herald

LIVE WIRE STRIPS CLOTHES
FROM ORGANIST IN STREET

Headline in *New York Times*

The Safety Director of Rhode Island, USA, finds it difficult to frame regulations controlling surfing. While surfers are on their boards they are under the jurisdiction of the State Division of Harbours and Rivers. When they fall off their boards they are the concern of the State Division of Parks and Recreation.

Reveille

BREAKS BOTH LEGS TURNING
OVER IN BED

Headline in *The World*

MRS KITTY CLARK BIRKS – I would like to communicate with you, object going 315 miles north with you.

GEORGE

The World

Will the person who unknown to me returned the family album, horseshoe ring, 72-inch pearl beads, 2 side combs set with brilliants, 36-inch pearl beads, PLEASE RETURN the 25th photograph of the condemned building corner Ivins and Oak Avenues, opposite city line. Reward. Apply – – – – –.

Advert in *Philadelphia Record*

Miss Yolande Messiter, sister of the bride, was maid of honour and wore a white ninon skirt, matching ostrich plumes in her hair and carried a royal blue brother of the bride, and Marcel. The bridegroom was attended by his velvet muff covered with pink roses.

Portland Press Herald

The Federal Communications Commission has advised that there is nothing in the law to prevent two licensed amateur radio stations being utilized to consummate a wedding ceremony between a couple separated by the Pacific Ocean.

from a press release

(I particularly like to hear from readers which items have pleased them most. My own favourites are those like the last item on page 121 which provide fruit for hours of head-scratching speculation.

My correspondence shows that there are now a great number of keen shrdlologists – many in Australia – and I welcome news of fresh exploits perpetrated by the inimitable Gobfrey Shrdlu. – D.P.)

Denys Parsons
Funny Convulsing and Funny Confusing £1.25

Rollicking new boners and bungles, gaffes and giggles. On the left-hand pages. Funny Convulsing – on the right, Funny Confusing. So take your pick of Denys Parsons – Mr Laughter Unlimited ...

The Best of Shrdlu £1

The irrepressible Shrdlu is that malicious spirit who lurks at the elbow of weary printers and journalists to produce such disastrous printed consequences as:

'Thieves stole 600 loaves a bread from an empty delivery van yesterday.'

'For Sale: Lovely rosewood piano. Owner going abroad with beautiful twisted legs.'

'Ghana is to change over to driving on the right. The change will be made gradually.'

Here is the cream of Shrdlology, culled from the bestselling *Funny* series, and accompanied by many brand-new gems.

edited by Fritz Spiegl
A Small Book of Grave Humour £1.25

'The object of an epitaph is to identify the resting place of the mortal remains of a dead person. It should therefore record only such information as is reasonably necessary for that purpose ...'
THE CHURCHYARD HANDBOOK

Thank Heaven the above injunction has not always been strictly observed – as witness the following examples from this touching, very funny collection:

'Here lies Lester Moore ... Four slugs from a 44 ... No less no more'

'Here lieth Mary, the wife of John Ford ... We hope her soul is gone to the Lord ... But if for Hell she has changed this life, she had better be there than be John Ford's wife'

edited by Fritz Spiegl
Dead Funny £1.50

'Beneath this sod lies another' – the long-awaited second Book of
Grave Humour from the ever-watchful Spiegl who, during the years
of success of his first collection of the funnier side of tombstones, *A
Small Book of Grave Humour*, has continued to collect mirthful
mementos mori and has now put together a second book which
promises to be every bit as popular as the first.

Rob Buckman
Jogging From Memory £1.25

Hangovers, insomnia, Sunday papers, Heidegger, hi-fi, Round Britain
Quizzes and why Ibsen's plays are really comic masterpieces – just
some of the topics dealt with by broadcasting's funniest doctor.
Thirty enlightening and hilarious essays from one of today's foremost
humourists, enhanced by the brilliant cartoons of Martin Honeysett
and concluding with an introduction from Dr Sigmund Freud
(deceased).

'If you don't bust a gut with laughter, you can sue me'
DR SIGMUND FREUD

Nicholas Parsons
Dipped in Vitriol £1.75

'Perception of badness, as of beauty, is in the eye of the beholder ...
This is a humorous excursion through the realms of badness,
highlighting self-importance in autobiography, pretentiousness and
incompetence in fiction, mountebankery and shallowness in theatre,
whimsical follies in music, brain-crushing false goods in cinema ...'
A hilarious survey of hatchet reviews of the arts through the epochs
– vitriolic offerings from Clive James, Bernard Levin, Gore Vidal,
Oscar Wilde, Richard Ingrams, the *Sun*, *Pravda*, George Bernard
Shaw and many more.

James Herriot
If Only They Could Talk £1.50

The genial misadventures of James Herriot, a young vet in the lovely
Yorkshire Dales, are enough to make a cat laugh – let alone the
animals, if only they could talk.

It Shouldn't Happen to a Vet £1.75

'Imagine a *Dr Finlay's Casebook* scripted by Richard Gordon and
Thurlow Craig and starring Ronnie Corbett and you will understand
why James Herriot is on to a winner ... a delightful new collection
of stories'
SUNDAY EXPRESS

Let Sleeping Vets Lie £1.50

The hilarious revelations of James Herriot, the now famous vet in the
Yorkshire Dales, continues his happy story of everyday trials and
tribulations with unwilling animal patients and their richly diverse
owners.

Vet in Harness £1.50

With the fourth of this superb series, James Herriot again takes us
on his varied and often hair-raising journeys to still more joyous
adventures in the Yorkshire Dales.

All Creatures Great and Small £2.95

The long-awaited first James Herriot volume, comprising *If Only
They Could Talk, It Shouldn't Happen to a Vet,* and also the
completed courtship of James and Helen from *Let Sleeping Vets Lie.*
A magnificent gift – for a friend or for yourself.

Fiction

☐	**Options**	Freda Bright	£1.50p
☐	**The Thirty-nine Steps**	John Buchan	£1.50p
☐	**Secret of Blackoaks**	Ashley Carter	£1.50p
☐	**Hercule Poirot's Christmas**	Agatha Christie	£1.25p
☐	**Dupe**	Liza Cody	£1.25p
☐	**Lovers and Gamblers**	Jackie Collins	£2.50p
☐	**Sphinx**	Robin Cook	£1.25p
☐	**Ragtime**	E. L. Doctorow	£1.50p
☐	**My Cousin Rachel**	Daphne du Maurier	£1.95p
☐	**Mr American**	George Macdonald Fraser	£2.25p
☐	**The Moneychangers**	Arthur Hailey	£2.25p
☐	**Secrets**	Unity Hall	£1.50p
☐	**Simon the Coldheart**	Georgette Heyer	95p
☐	**The Eagle Has Landed**	Jack Higgins	£1.95p
☐	**Sins of the Fathers**	Susan Howatch	£2.95p
☐	**The Master Sniper**	Stephen Hunter	£1.50p
☐	**Smiley's People**	John le Carré	£1.95p
☐	**To Kill a Mockingbird**	Harper Lee	£1.75p
☐	**Ghosts**	Ed McBain	£1.75p
☐	**Gone with the Wind**	Margaret Mitchell	£3.50p
☐	**The Totem**	David Morrell	£1.25p
☐	**Platinum Logic**	Tony Parsons	£1.75p
☐	**Wilt**	Tom Sharpe	£1.50p
☐	**Rage of Angels**	Sidney Sheldon	£1.75p
☐	**The Unborn**	David Shobin	£1.50p
☐	**A Town Like Alice**	Nevile Shute	£1.75p
☐	**A Falcon Flies**	Wilbur Smith	£1.95p
☐	**The Deep Well at Noon**	Jessica Stirling	£1.95p
☐	**The Ironmaster**	Jean Stubbs	£1.75p
☐	**The Music Makers**	E. V. Thompson	£1.95p

Non-fiction

☐	**Extraterrestrial Civilizations**	Isaac Asimov	£1.50p
☐	**Pregnancy**	Gordon Bourne	£2.95p
☐	**Jogging From Memory**	Rob Buckman	£1.25p
☐	**The 35mm Photographer's Handbook**	Julian Calder and John Garrett	£5.95p
☐	**Travellers' Britain**	Arthur Eperon	£2.95p
☐	**Travellers' Italy**		£2.50p
☐	**The Complete Calorie Counter**	Eileen Fowler	75p

☐	**The Diary of Anne Frank**	Anne Frank	£1.50p
☐	**And the Walls Came Tumbling Down**	Jack Fishman	£1.95p
☐	**Linda Goodman's Sun Signs**	Linda Goodman	£2.50p
☐	**On the House**	Simon Hoggart	£1.50p
☐	**How to be a Gifted Parent**	David Lewis	£1.95p
☐	**Victoria RI**	Elizabeth Longford	£4.95p
☐	**Symptoms**	Sigmund Stephen Miller	£2.50p
☐	**Book of Worries**	Robert Morley	£1.50p
☐	**Airport International**	Brian Moynahan	£1.75p
☐	**The Alternative Holiday Catalogue**	edited by Harriet Peacock	£1.95p
☐	**The Pan Book of Card Games**	Hubert Phillips	£1.75p
☐	**Food for All the Family**	Magnus Pyke	£1.50p
☐	**Just Off for the Weekend**	John Slater	£2.50p
☐	**An Unfinished History of the World**	Hugh Thomas	£3.95p
☐	**The Baby and Child Book**	Penny and Andrew Stanway	£4.95p
☐	**The Third Wave**	Alvin Toffler	£1.95p
☐	**Pauper's Paris**	Miles Turner	£2.50p
☐	**The Flier's Handbook**		£5.95p

All these books are available at your local bookshop or newsagent, or can be ordered direct from the publisher. Indicate the number of copies required and fill in the form below   8

....

Name_____
(Block letters please)

Address_____

_____

Send to Pan Books (CS Department), Cavaye Place, London SW10 9PG
Please enclose remittance to the value of the cover price plus:
35p for the first book plus 15p per copy for each additional book ordered
to a maximum charge of £1.25 to cover postage and packing
Applicable only in the UK

While every effort is made to keep prices low, it is sometimes
necessary to increase prices at short notice. Pan Books reserve
the right to show on covers and charge new retail prices which
may differ from those advertised in the text or elsewhere